REDISCOVER T...
OF NATURE W...

THE SCIENCE AND ART...
Tom Brown shares the wis... ...ge...
—revelations that awaken us to our own place in nature and in the world

THE TRACKER
Tom Brown's classic true story—the most powerful and magical high-spiritual adventure since *The Teachings of Don Juan*

THE SEARCH
The continuing story of *The Tracker*, exploring the ancient art of the new survival

THE VISION
Tom Brown's profound, personal journey into an ancient mystical experience, the Vision Quest

THE QUEST
The acclaimed outdoorsman shows how we can save our planet

THE JOURNEY
A message of hope and harmony for our earth and our spirits—Tom Brown's vision for healing our world

GRANDFATHER
The incredible true story of a remarkable Native American and his lifelong search for peace and truth in nature

AWAKENING SPIRITS
For the first time, Tom Brown shares the unique meditation exercises used by students of his personal Tracker classes

THE WAY OF THE SCOUT
Tom Brown's newest, most empowering work—a collection of stories illustrating the advanced tracking skills taught to him by Grandfather

**AND THE BESTSELLING SERIES
OF TOM BROWN'S FIELD GUIDES**

ABOUT THE AUTHOR

At the age of eight, Tom Brown, Jr., began to learn tracking and hunting from Stalking Wolf, a displaced Apache Indian. Today Brown is an experienced woodsman whose extraordinary skill has saved many lives, including his own. He manages and teaches one of the largest wilderness and survival schools in the U.S. and has instructed many law enforcement agencies and rescue teams.

Awakening
Spirits

TOM BROWN, JR.

BERKLEY BOOKS, NEW YORK

THE BERKLEY PUBLISHING GROUP
Published by the Penguin Group
Penguin Group (USA) Inc.
375 Hudson Street, New York, New York 10014, USA
Penguin Group (Canada), 90 Eglinton Avenue East, Suite 700, Toronto, Ontario M4P 2Y3, Canada
(a division of Pearson Penguin Canada Inc.)
Penguin Books Ltd., 80 Strand, London WC2R 0RL, England
Penguin Group Ireland, 25 St. Stephen's Green, Dublin 2, Ireland (a division of Penguin Books Ltd.)
Penguin Group (Australia), 250 Camberwell Road, Camberwell, Victoria 3124, Australia
(a division of Pearson Australia Group Pty. Ltd.)
Penguin Books India Pvt. Ltd., 11 Community Centre, Panchsheel Park, New Delhi—110 017, India
Penguin Group (NZ), 67 Apollo Drive, Mairangi Bay, Auckland 1311, New Zealand
(a division of Pearson New Zealand Ltd.)
Penguin Books (South Africa) (Pty.) Ltd., 24 Sturdee Avenue, Rosebank, Johannesburg 2196,
South Africa

Penguin Books Ltd., Registered Offices: 80 Strand, London WC2R 0RL, England

A Berkley Book / published by arrangement with the author

The publisher does not have any control over and does not assume any responsibility for author or
third-party websites or their content.

AWAKENING SPIRITS

PRINTING HISTORY
Berkley trade paperback edition / April 1994

ISBN: 0-425-14140-3

PRINTED IN THE UNITED STATES OF AMERICA

30 29 28 27 26 25 24 23 22

Most Berkley Books are available at special quantity discounts for bulk purchases for sales
promotions, premiums, fund-raising, or educational use. Special books, or book excerpts,
can also be created to fit specific needs.

For details, write: Special Markets, The Berkley Publishing Group, 375 Hudson Street, New York,
New York 10014.

Contents

Preface

It is with great trepidation that I embark on the journey of writing this book. Yes, I am concerned that the reader will possibly have a difficult time trying to learn the concepts and techniques that I set forth. After all, the book basically covers the spiritual skills learned by my students in my basic philosophy workshops taught at my school, and I worry that something may be lost in the translation between teaching the class physically and learning through the written word. However, I still have hope. Thinking back, nearly a decade ago, I remember having the same worries about writing the field guides, wondering whether the reader could actually learn from the written word. Over the years, and to my amazement, I found that people can not only learn from these field guides but actually master the skills. It is with this hope that I begin writing.

This book is basically written in three parts. The first part tells the story of how Grandfather, Stalking Wolf, arrived at the basic philosophy; the second part deals with how I learned the basic techniques and skills of the spirit; and the final part teaches the reader how to integrate them into his daily life. After all, what good is a philosophy and the power of the spirit if one cannot use it on a constant daily basis? I know that if the reader dedicates himself to the learning of the techniques at hand, practices regularly, and approaches these techniques with open enthusiasm, then he will not only excel but master these techniques. The same holds true with any how-to book, regardless of the topic.

One of my greatest concerns, however, is the way that the reader approaches and understands the concepts. As I just said, first there must be an enthusiasm and openness, but second, there must be a basic acceptance, thus the source of my worry. You see, much of what I teach and write concerning the spirit has no scientific or technological proof system. I must rely then solely on reproducible results and grand miracles that are evident every day. Thus the reader will build his or her own belief system. But I must say here what I tell the students in all of my classes: "If you believe everything I say, then you are a fool. Your job is not to believe me, but to prove me right or prove me wrong." That, essentially, is what Grandfather demanded of me when he taught me these skills. He did not want me to accept these things at face value, but to make them work for me and become part of my daily reality.

Another problem and concern I have with writing this book is the wealth of spiritual information found in countless other books and video programs, not to mention classes on the subject. Unfortunately much of the information presented to the general public is a myth, or at best works only intermittently and poorly. Yes, this book may challenge the very core of your belief systems and shake up your personal philosophy, but that is not my intent. What I set forth in this book is not meant to degrade what you believe, but to enhance and magnify those beliefs. Simply, the techniques and skills can be easily integrated into all philosophies, religions, and belief systems. After all, Grandfather considered these teachings the common thread that runs through all things.

To tell you the truth, I did not really want to write this book. I felt that these things could only be taught in a workshop situation where I could guide the process personally and be there to answer questions. I also thought that a student must complete my basic standard class before he or she could tackle the concepts of my philosophy workshops, but I am finding that this is not true. It was not I that initiated the writing of this book, but the urging of thousands of my students who have completed my philosophy workshops. They felt that the book was needed, stating that it would reach far more people than I could by just teaching classes on a physical level. Their argument is that there is only one of me, and the information contained in the philosophy class is sorely needed today.

So it is with these things in mind that I begin to write this book. Yes, I am concerned about the results. I know that when I physically teach a class the results are nothing short of miraculous. I watch students of every faith walk away from my school spellbound by what they are able to do and the way they communicate with the world of nature and spirit. I have had priests, ministers, theologians, and countless others from almost all religions and philosophies gain the same enlightening results as the layperson. I know that it works for all people, for I have seen the results firsthand. I think that it is summed up best by a dear friend, Father J., who is a Catholic priest. He said to me after his first philosophy class, "This is what I was looking for. Now I can understand my beliefs fully. It was only after taking this class that I realized what we teach and do in church is worship, but what I learned here is spirituality. I know now there is a deep chasm between worship and spirituality, and my job now is to bring them together and teach the masses."

Whenever possible, especially in the latter part of this book, I use my students' experiences to demonstrate a particular point or spiritual teaching. These people have shown me that Grandfather's teaching and philosophy works for everyone and anyone. It makes no difference if that person is highly religious or atheist or everything in between. It works for everyone. This book, however, is not the beginning and the end of Grandfather's teachings. I could write volumes to say the least. Also, I am not a leader or guru, but a student of the spirit, just as yourself. I make no claims to be better, for each person possesses his or her own unique power. There is no church or cathedral in the things I set forth, for the only church is the wilderness, that which the Creator made. There is no leader other than your own heart. You are unique and the way you use this information will be unique. Thus there is no one more or less powerful, just equal and splendidly different. Empty your cup and you will learn. Approach this book like a child and you will understand and become "one" with earth and spirit, as Grandfather taught. Simply, welcome to Grandfather's world.

Finally, I can take absolutely no credit for anything written in this book. It all belongs to Grandfather, Stalking Wolf. After all, he was the one who dedicated his entire life and endless wandering to the quest of finding the "basic and pure truth." I would love to be the author of these techniques and concepts, but I do not possess that kind of genius. I only wish that I did. I am but a signpost, a parrot, and a guide of that philosophy, not its originator. It belongs to everyone. It is the basic common thread and purity that runs through all philosophies and religions. It belongs to everyone and no one.

Introduction

I cannot assume that everyone who reads this book has read any of my other books, thus this book must stand on its own. It is important here that I present a brief history of Grandfather's life and teachings, as well as the decade he spent with me in his later years. After all, it is the basic foundation of my skills and subsequently my school and the birth of the philosophy that I teach there. I see the real birth of all of this beginning at the dawn of man, when people lived close to the earth and the Creator. It is common to us all, no matter where we come from or what we now believe. It is the basic foundation of all our beliefs, now obscured with all the customs, traditions, ceremonies, and doctrines. Out of all this dusty complication walked the man Stalking Wolf, whom I call Grandfather.

Grandfather was born in southwestern Texas, to a small group of Apache people. His little clan, fearing the Whites and Mexicans, wandered far away from the rest of their people, hoping to keep themselves, their beliefs, and their lifestyle intact. His small band of people lived the nomadic life of the hunter and gatherer, secretly avoiding any encounter with hostile forces by living in the most rugged conditions known on earth. Unfortunately, this lifestyle was short-lived, for Grandfather's parents and grandparents were slaughtered by Mexican forces near the border when he was just two years old. Fortunately for Grandfather, his Great-grandfather, Coyote Thunder, and a handful of people escaped with him to the rugged mountain deserts of Mexico. There he would spend the next twenty years of his life.

Though there was no real chief or elected leader of the group, Coyote Thunder was looked upon as the sage or elder, thus giving him status as a leader of sorts. Coyote Thunder despised the ways of the White man and forbade anyone in his clan to use any manufactured tool. He believed that to keep his small group of people safe from the influences of the Whites, they would have to remain true to their beliefs and their ancient lifestyle. There was nothing in the world outside of the wilderness that Coyote Thunder or his people needed. He wanted them to live a pure life, free from all worldly distractions, and seek the spiritual life rather than a life oriented in the flesh. This became the group consciousness, a general consensus without dispute. Most in the group were elders anyway and long ago had grown weary of the flesh. It was these elders who would have the greatest influence on Grandfather.

Grandfather was first schooled in the practical skills of the camp, taught mainly by the women of the group. He then became a skilled hunter, providing meat to many who could not hunt. He also became a master herbalist, taught by an old medicine woman who was a close friend of Coyote Thunder. Most of all, Grandfather became one of the best scouts of the group. He mastered the art of invisible walking and invisibility. He could survive easily where so many others would perish, and he became the best tracker that Coyote Thunder had ever known. So, too, was his skill in awareness, for the elders said that they knew of no one who had keener senses. Before the age of twenty, Grandfather became legendary, not only to his own people, but to many outside his tribe. Even hearing his name would strike worry in the white community, though Grandfather had done nothing to merit this fear in others. He detested killing and war.

But beyond all of the physical skills that Grandfather had mastered, his passion was for the ways of the spirit. Since as far back as he could remember, he had profound communications with the world of nature and of spirit. Even when he was a young teen, many came to him for herbal remedies. By his mid-teens he was considered a sage and a shaman. His ability and mastery of the wisdom of the spirit shocked even the most liberal-minded elder. Many of the elders believed that Grandfather was given a special gift from the Creator and was above common man. But Grandfather did not believe that for one minute, for he did nothing that anyone else could not do. He was always humble around everyone. Spiritual arrogance was beyond his conception.

In his early twenties Grandfather left his people due to a series of visions and dreams that he experienced during childhood. These visions and dreams told him to go forth and learn as much as he could of the old ways and preserve them. The visions also told him to teach what he knew and to lead people back to the earth and a life of simplicity. He was guided to live the ascetic life, free from all worldly possessions, and as always alone. Most of all the visions guided his life to the wisdom of the spirit. His was a quest to learn as much as he could of all the religions, philosophies, and beliefs of man, find the common thread, and simplify. He was to seek the common and pure truth. It was these visions and dreams that demanded he wander alone in his search for nearly sixty-three years.

Before he reached his mid-twenties, Grandfather had transcended all of his basic religious beliefs and now walked what he considered the simple path of purity. He traveled extensively and relentlessly. His journeys took him to the far reaches of Alaska, throughout Canada, many times across the United States, through Central America, and even to the southernmost tip of Argentina. He traveled without time or destination, without the need for anyone outside of himself and nature. He lived the simple and ascetic life of a wanderer. His only guide, his only direction, came from the driving force of his Inner Vision and the dictates of the spirit world. With each passing year his knowledge of the old ways grew. So, too, did his knowledge of the religions of man. It was these that he simplified and purified, tested and practiced, until all complications and dogmas were stripped away.

I met Grandfather when he was eighty-three and I barely seven. For over ten years he became the greatest influence in my life. He taught me the ways of survival and the philosophy of living with the earth so that I, too, could go out into the wilderness with nothing. He taught me to track and observe as a scout, where my awareness would become as good if not better than the average scout. But most of all he taught me his basic and simple philosophy of life and spirit. I not only practiced them but lived them and found in them a profound truth which transcended all religion and philosophy. I learned to communicate with the world of nature and the realms of spirit in a very real and dynamic way, so that I began to walk the duality of flesh and spirit as Grandfather had done. So, too, did I develop a passion for seeking the basic spiritual truths.

After Grandfather left me and went back to his people, I wandered on and off for nearly ten years. I traveled extensively and tracked lost people for the police whenever possible, building my reputation as a tracker. I tested my skills of survival, tracking, and awareness in every conceivable environment to see if these techniques would keep me alive and comfortable. Many times I lived the secret life of the scout, existing without detection right next to the civilizations of man. Most of all I tested the skills of the spirit and continued the search for the simple truth and the ultimate enlightenment. In all of these years all I could do was to prove Grandfather right. I added very little to what he found except to find ways to teach them quickly to anyone who was seeking spiritual truth.

As Grandfather had prophesied so long ago, I eventually started a school and became an author. My school now has sixteen levels of classes covering all aspects of survival, tracking, awareness, and the philosophy of spirit, and I have educated nearly twenty thousand students; this will also be my fourteenth book. My students have become my best salespeople. Ninety percent of my new students are sent to the school by graduates. Ironically, the philosophy classes have become the most popular, and we find ourselves booking these sometimes months and even years in advance. I pride myself in teaching a philosophy that works and works for everyone, with dynamic and miraculous results. But like Grandfather did for me, all I can do is give students the tools they need to learn with—the rest is up to them. This book then becomes the tool and the way. What you do with it is up to you.

PART ONE

QUEST
FOR PURITY

It all began with Grandfather's Great-grandfather Coyote Thunder. Throughout his life Coyote Thunder was a highly spiritual man, a sage, and a religious leader of his small band of people, though not what we would consider to be a chief. Since his earliest recollection, he grew dissatisfied with his own basic belief, for he felt that there had to be much more. He first began to pick apart and purify his own beliefs by setting aside all the customs, traditions, and dogmas and finding what the basis of those beliefs really was. He told no one of what he was doing in those early years for fear of being ridiculed by the tribal elders. Though he took part in many of the ceremonies, he still knew that there was a faster and purer way to the purity of the spirit world.

Throughout his life he took many journeys away from his people, searching out first other "friendly" Native American tribes and learning the similarities and differences between their religions. Whenever possible, though with great fear, he would also search out the White man's religions. These encounters were rather infrequent, for any approach to the White man could have meant imprisonment or even death. As always, he took what he had witnessed and learned back to the cathedrals of nature to test it out or decipher its deeper and purer meanings. Unfortunately, much of what he learned just did not work in the world of creation and certainly did not work for everyone.

In his latter years Coyote Thunder found it became very dangerous to wander away from his people. Most of the time was spent moving and hiding from the White man, the Mexicans, and many other people who would kill his people at first sight. It was at this time, too, that he began to hear of broken treaties and of vast prisons called reservations, where people were treated like animals. Many Native Americans that were put on these reservations died of starvation and exposure. Many were converted to the White man's religion, and none were permitted to practice their religion or use the ancient skills. Coyote Thunder vowed never to allow his people to be imprisoned, and being that he hated war and killing, he kept his people constantly and secretly moving, avoiding being detected at all costs. He yearned to go out and continue his work of learning the religions and realities of man, but keeping his people safe took precedence. He was old now, and even if he had the chance, he would not be able to travel as he did in his youth.

He felt very saddened by the fact that so many native peoples were denied their freedom, and sadder still was the fact that many of the old ways and beliefs would be lost. He felt that he had been denied part of his Vision, for it was told to him during his first Vision Quest that he should wander and seek the purity of nature and spirit. The encroachment of the White man had destroyed his Vision, but he held hope that somehow he would be able to fulfill his destiny. Little did he know that his influence would do just that. Though he would be denied that quest for purity, he would sow the seed that would guide another to take up the work where he left off. After all, it was just as important to pass on a Vision as it was to live it fully.

1

The Seed

Coyote Thunder's dreams and Vision came true when he adopted and began to raise Grandfather, Stalking Wolf. Even when Grandfather was still a child, Great-grandfather Coyote Thunder saw something special in him. Stalking Wolf seemed to possess a deeper sense of the spirit, more so than the other children, and Coyote Thunder began to nurture this gift. He did not push Grandfather, but allowed him to seek the wisdom of the spirit by his own choosing. All Coyote Thunder did was to sow the seed in the fertile soil of Grandfather's heart. As Grandfather grew older, Coyote Thunder began to realize that his quest for spiritual purity would not die. Grandfather would finish the Vision that Coyote Thunder began.

From Grandfather's earliest memory, he could remember the many stories of Coyote Thunder's wanderings in his search for spiritual purity. Grandfather could not remember when he first began to feel the passions to wander and explore, especially for the spiritual purity that Coyote Thunder so often spoke. Yet there was a series of very powerful

dreams and visions that Grandfather received when he was
a young teen that began to make his quest for purity a real
driving force in his life. These prophetic dreams and visions
all seemed to come at once, over a period of a full cycle of
the moon. Grandfather said that each night there would be
dreams that drove him, and often there would be powerful
visions that would come from nowhere. He began to refer
to that month in his life as the moon of spiritual purity, for
it was the basis of all his searching for the rest of his life.

The first vision to seek spiritual purity came to Grandfather
in a very profound dream during his travels. He had wandered
far away from camp, exploring the northernmost regions for
possible encampments for his people. He had wandered out
of the most arid deserts where his people now collected
plants, and moved into the higher, more mountainous and
rugged elevations. He was hoping to find a winter camp
area that afforded protection from the winter storms and
from the eye of his people's enemies. He knew that in
these mountains he could find a small valley, much like
the camp area they had used for many previous winters.
His searching was important to the people of the tribe, for
their previous winter camp area had now been taken over by
a handful of White prospectors and a few trappers. It would
no longer provide a safe haven for winter. Now he, like the
other scouts, was secretly combing the mountains for new
locations.

Grandfather had been wandering for many days without
much success when he accidently found a perfect location,
better than he could ever imagine. He had passed by the small
hidden bowl-shaped valley a day earlier, but even with his
close proximity, he failed to notice it. In fact, he would have
passed it right by if he had not stopped to camp on the upper
lip of the canyon. Once his camp was made for the evening,
he relaxed before a small campfire. He was confident that
his fire would never be detected by the White man, for he
was too high up in the range and in very rugged terrain. He
knew the White man preferred to wander trails and roads,
and he was many miles from any trails, hundreds of miles

from any White man camps. As the evening began to grow quiet, he felt a deep peace wash over him as he slipped in and out of sleep.

Suddenly Grandfather sprang to his feet and cupped his hands to his ears, straining to catch the sounds from the distant canyon. There was no mistaking the sound, it was flowing water, barely audible even in the still of the evening. His eyes strained in the waning light for the origin of the sound, but the landscape would not give up its secret. He knew that the sound was coming from the center of the vast canyon that stretched before him, but it refused to reveal its location. He searched the distant snowy mountain peaks to find the origins of the stream, but not a ribbon of water was visible, at least none that flowed to the center of the canyon. He wondered if it were not some sort of ventriloquial water song, originating from a distant stream and echoing off the canyon walls. After all, it was common along these rugged peaks for sound to be distorted and echoed. He decided to get a full night's sleep and head into the canyon at first light.

Try as he might, Grandfather could not sleep. As soon as he neared the edge of sleep, he would hear the faint song of the stream. He began to argue with his heart. One part of him wanted to go to sleep and search the canyon in the morning, for it was too rugged and treacherous to search the area at night. The bigger part of him, however, wanted to immediately begin the journey into the heart of the canyon. Without regard to the hazards of the rugged terrain or the darkness, he left his camp. The call to find the stream was far too powerful. It was more than a call. It was a spiritual beckoning, a demand, that he knew all too well. There was no hesitation or thought for his own safety, for he knew without a doubt that his spirit would guide him as it had on countless other similar journeys and quests.

He picked his way carefully down the steep and rocky slope of the canyon, being careful not to dislodge any rocks that could cause a landslide. At first the going was very difficult, for he had to literally feel his way down the rocks, not only with his feet but most of the time with his hands also.

His progress was very slow, especially as he neared what he assumed to be the halfway point, though he could not really tell. This part of the trip demanded that he back down in a crawl position, not that it mattered, because he could not see anyway. On a flat ledge he sat down to rest and looked back up the canyon slope, now accented by the sky. As he began to make out the rocky crags and steep rock-strewn slopes, he felt that even in daylight it would have been a difficult climb. He wondered if there might be an easier route for his people.

As Grandfather lay resting, the moon slowly began to rise over the lip of the canyon. It cast the whole area into an eerie glow. Rocks, boulders, and jagged peaks cast deep shadows that seemed to shift before his eyes, but now the area would be much easier to travel. So, too, from his lofty position, could Grandfather now see the faint, silvery sparkle of the distant stream that first beckoned him. To his amazement it seemed to pour directly from the face of the cliff, with no visible tributary in sight. Could it be, he thought, that the spring runs off the snowmelt, then disappears underground, only to emerge in this hidden canyon many miles from its origin? He wondered where the stream went from the canyon floor, and if this place would be safe for his people after all. He knew that streams would create an easy access for anyone, especially "those who lust for gold." It was the streams that these White men seemed to seek, and this stream would be a tremendous find for them.

Now with the moon fully in the sky, his trip went quickly and easily. By the time the moon was approaching the opposite canyon wall, he found a second canyon, deep inside the first. With the last remaining moonlight he could clearly see all the way to the bottom. The small stream cut the canyon floor in half like a silvery ribbon, and on each side of the stream were lush forests and fields. There was no sign that anyone had ever been there. There were no native encampments and certainly no White man's shantytowns. He breathed a deep sigh of relief and was suddenly struck by a deep sense of wonder as the beauty of the valley filtered through to his spirit. He knew without a doubt that this area would provide one of the finest and most protected winter camps that he had ever known, provided that there was no easy, hidden, secret entrance. Now, even more than before, the spiritual calling, coupled with intense excitement, beckoned him down to the canyon floor.

As he went over the lip of the second canyon, the moonlight disappeared from its face. Only a portion of the canyon floor far below was washed in moonlight, but that was disappearing fast. He again had to revert to a reverse crawl, taking even more care than before, as now this canyon wall was much steeper than the first. The sky began to grow light before he reached the floor, and not soon enough, for the last part of the climb was very treacherous and the steepest he had yet encountered. As soon as the ground flattened out, he lay down to rest on the rich soil of the canyon floor. This ground was so fertile and soft that he likened it to floating on water. So alive was this area that he could almost feel it breathe. The earth here seemed so vibrant, pure, and energized.

The flat outer edge of the canyon, with its tall trees and lush underbrush, gave way to a field that gently sloped to the water's edge. At the upper end of the field, the land flattened and there would be an excellent place for a camp. From the edge of the field, Grandfather had a full view of the entire canyon and saw that at the far end, near the origin of the stream, was an easier access. He knew that the elders of the tribe would have no problem descending the slopes at this point. The area was perfect. Not only was the great canyon far away and inaccessible to most people, but even if it were discovered, one would not see the smaller inner canyon. Here his people would be safe for the winter, and probably throughout the year if they wanted. There was enough of everything—food, water, firewood, and plenty of shelter building materials. The outer canyon would provide additional excellent hunting.

Now Grandfather began to wander upstream. He was in no hurry to get back to his people, for it normally could have taken months to find such a location. Right away he wanted to explore and confirm the origin of the stream. It still appeared to flow right from a rocky area on the steepest side of the canyon. Even from his vantage point in the field, he could see no evidence of any stream feeding the canyon stream, nor did he know where the stream flowed out of the canyon. As he approached the origin of the little stream, his suspicions were proven. It appeared to seep from the side of the canyon from several small springs, where it collected in a small pond. From here it cascaded down a small rocky cliff, formed another small pool, then flowed across the little canyon. Now all Grandfather needed to do was to check how the stream made its exit.

It did not take long for Grandfather to find where the stream left the little canyon. Near the far wall, nearly hidden by tall trees, the little stream poured down a steep boulder-strewn ravine, which was also hidden by tall trees and very thick vegetation. It not only cut through the little canyon, but cut right through the larger canyon. Such was the steepness and ruggedness of the ravine that no one would ever attempt to climb up. Grandfather knew that the ravine faced one of the most inaccessible wilderness areas, and there would be no White men there for a very long time. Here was a gift from the Creator. This place was just perfect for his people, and there was no doubt in Grandfather's mind that they would love to live here. He could not understand, however, why his people had never found this place before. Yes, he was a long way from the main camp, but certainly someone from his tribe would know of its whereabouts. He then had the thought, and subsequently the fear, that this place might be sacred, or possibly evil. Yet his heart spoke otherwise. He decided to camp in the area for a few days, to explore, and to search the canyon spirit.

Without hesitation, Grandfather began to build his camp in the flat field, where he knew his people would probably build the main camp. At least from there he could try it out and get to know the personality of the area, the stream, and the canyon itself. So, too, did he hope for rain, to see if the area might flood, or the stream turn murky.

After his camp was built, the fatigue from lack of sleep and the intense journey into the canyon caught up with Grandfather. He was laying on a thick carpet of moss near the little pool at the base of the waterfall when he fell into a sound sleep. The next thing he remembered was awakening to the sound of the stream and the moonlight. He had no idea what had awakened him, perhaps a calling of some sort, but he did not remember. He was still very tired and arose to go back to his shelter, but he felt so numb and cold that he could barely stand. It seemed to take forever for Grandfather to get his balance and bearings, and walking was nearly impossible. It was as if something were holding him there and he could not move. So, too, did he feel a little dizzy, and giving in to the feeling, he sat back down on the ground. He was puzzled by his fatigue, for he had gone without sleep many times before and never felt this way.

He gazed into the little pond as his mind raced to find the answers to his profound fatigue and inability to move. In the moonlight he could see right into the bottom of the pond, and except for the ripples and concentric rings there appeared to be no water at all. Suddenly he heard the calling again and looked up from the stream to the distant bank. There on the other side, barely visible in the moonlight, stood an old woman. She stood absolutely motionless, eyeing Grandfather. Grandfather returned the gaze in utter disbelief. She made no attempt to move closer to Grandfather or make any kind of retreat. She seemed very confident and unafraid of Grandfather. Grandfather began to feel a little self-conscious and a little fearful, such was the power he felt in this old woman. The moon cast a faint halo as it reflected across her white hair, making her appear as some sort of deity. Grandfather remained speechless.

Deftly the old woman slipped into the blackness of the thick woods. Grandfather never saw her take a step or turn; instead, she just slowly disappeared into the silence. He shook his head to determine if the image of the woman was real or just the play of moonlight and shadow, but no image returned. Suddenly Grandfather had the sense that something was watching him from the far side of the little clearing. Turning abruptly, he again saw the old woman, standing just a few yards away from him. Grandfather asked her who she was, in a very hoarse and fear-choked voice. The old woman did not answer, nor did she move. Instead, she just stood there watching Grandfather. Grandfather again tried to stand, but his legs felt heavy, as if they were asleep. Fear now bordered on panic, for he assumed that this woman was using some powerful medicine to hold him there.

Grandfather called to her again, and this time the old one moved closer to him. He could see now that she was very old, older than he had first thought, yet there was no indication of her great age in the way she walked. Instead, she walked as a young woman should. Without a pause, she asked Grandfather in a very firm voice what he was doing in her canyon. Grandfather explained to the old woman that his people needed to find a safe place for the winter, and he was one of the scouts sent to find a place. He also told her that he was sorry for intruding on her property, and he would leave at first light. There was no immediate response from the old woman, just a painful silence that seemed to last forever. Grandfather continued to try to make conversation with the old one, telling her how beautiful her canyon was and how very lucky she was to live in such a place.

There was still no response from the old woman, and Grandfather began to grow even more uneasy, not only because he still could not move but also because the old one would not speak. Finally the old woman broke the silence and said, "I care not that your people live in my canyon. Your people live close to the earth, and I know that they will take care of my place. I also know your Great-grandfather, Coyote Thunder, for I taught him when he was very young. You may have heard of me. I am 'Grandmother of the plants,' and I know that Coyote Thunder has probably mentioned me." Grandfather's head seemed to surge with utter disbelief. He had heard many stories of this old woman. It was she who had taught Coyote Thunder to be an herbalist. She was legendary and greatly respected by all the elders of his clan. But she had also passed away into the spirit plane many years before Grandfather was born. Now she stood before him, and he was humbled and spellbound.

Before Grandfather could utter a word, she said, "Now that you have found my beautiful and sacred valley, what are you still doing here?" Grandfather told her that he wanted to find out if this place was truly a great home for his people. She retorted, saying, "What does your heart say? Has not Coyote Thunder taught you to listen to your Inner Vision? If you listened to the stories that Coyote Thunder told you, you would know of this place, for he has been here many times. This is where I taught him." It was then that Grandfather realized that this was the valley Coyote Thunder and many other elders had so often alluded to. He also knew that they would not come here to live, out of respect for the old woman's spirit. Before Grandfather could speak, the old one said, "Tell him that it is good that he comes here. It will keep him safe for many years. I know of his plight and fear of the White man." She then slipped a fossil shell necklace from her neck and handed it to Grandfather. She spoke again, saying, "Give him this and he will know that you speak the truth."

Grandfather gazed at the necklace in his trembling hands. He could not believe that the spirit of the old woman had appeared to him. He felt so unworthy. She had been such a powerful shaman and herbalist when she was alive, and now only the old ones could talk to her. She only appeared to those she had taught, and only during times of dire need. He could not believe that she spoke to him, far less appeared before him, and even more amazed that she had given him the necklace. He was awestruck to silence. She then smiled warmly, knowing that he felt unworthy, and spoke to him softly, saying, "Great-grandson, you are not unworthy. Your task is great and you need guidance from the spirit world to find the purity which you seek." Without waiting for an answer, she continued, "I know that you know I speak the truth, though you have only begun to feel the yearnings to find the spiritual truth, the simplicity, that is the basis of all beliefs and religions. You have yearned to finish the work that Coyote Thunder started many years ago, but you fear for your people and you will not leave them."

There was a long moment of silence, a silence that allowed Grandfather to reflect on what the old one was telling him, and she spoke the truth. It was as if she could look directly into the deepest places of his heart and spirit and know his deepest yearnings. He could not deny what she had told him. She continued, saying, "Your people will be safe for a long time in this place, and you will then be free to wander as Coyote Thunder did. You must seek the purity of spirit at all costs, for that is what is most important. Mankind, living now far from the earth and spirit, complicates and distorts spiritual truth. The religions and philosophies of man grow more corrupted and complicated every day. With that distortion there will come a great dissatisfaction, and man will ultimately move away from spirit and dwell only in the flesh. His spirit will become imprisoned in the flesh. You must not delay your quest, for time is running out for man and our Earth Mother."

With those words she vanished into the night, and Grandfather found himself lying on the bed of moss, awakening to the dawn sky. He was shocked to realize that it had all been a dream, yet it felt so real. He sat up, blinking his eyes in the bright light and stretching to get the stiffness out of his back. It was then that he felt something in his hand. He looked in utter amazement at the old necklace the old woman had given to him. He did not know how it all had happened. He did not remember falling back to sleep after the old woman had departed, but he would not allow himself the luxury of any more questions. That is the way of the spirit world, and he grew accustomed to that kind of lucid Vision long ago. All he knew now was that he had to get back to Coyote Thunder and his people as fast as he could, not only to tell them that it was all right to live in the canyon, but also what the old woman had told him.

Though Grandfather took seven days to complete the journey the first time, it took him only three days to return to his village, such was his determination to get back. Throughout the entire trek back to his people, all Grandfather could think about was what the old woman had said. There was no doubt in his mind that he had truly encountered her, and what she told him of his quest for spiritual purity was truth. She did not tell him anything he did not know about his quest, only confirmed what he should be doing. However, he still felt unworthy of such a task, and still feared leaving his people for very long without his help. He was the youngest of the tribe and provided many with food and helped with the overall protection. There was a deep conflict brewing inside of him, and he had to get to Coyote Thunder quickly, before he talked himself out of his quest.

As Grandfather approached camp, Coyote Thunder and several elders met him. Without saying a word they scrutinized him very carefully, almost with an attitude of amazement and disbelief. Before Grandfather could say a word, Coyote Thunder said, "You have found the canyon, Grandson," which was more of a statement of fact than a question. The other elders announced their agreement with Coyote Thunder's words. Grandfather felt very self-conscious, as if he had broken some unspoken law. He could not understand how they knew by just looking at him. Certainly he was different, but the change had occurred deep inside him. Coyote Thunder spoke again and said, "I can tell by the look in your eyes, Grandson, that not only have you been to the sacred canyon, but you have seen the old one. Tell me, Grandson, what did she have to say to you? We have not seen her for many winters."

Grandfather hesitated at first, fearing that the crowd of elders was too much for him to bear. He wanted to talk to Coyote Thunder alone, but now he had to face them all. Still concerned that he had violated some law, he spoke very shyly and said, "Grandmother Plant told me that it was all right for the People to live in her canyon. She said that she knew of our plight and that we would be safe there for a long time." With that Grandfather sheepishly handed the fossil shell necklace to Coyote Thunder. Coyote Thunder stared at the necklace thoughtfully, trying to hide his amazement and joy from Grandfather. He lifted his eyes to meet Grandfather and said without turning to the elders, "The Wolf speaks the truth," but his eyes never left Grandfather. Stalking Wolf could feel Coyote Thunder's searching gaze, which remained upon him even after the elders had left. Coyote Thunder then said, in an anxious whisper, "And what else did she tell you?"

Grandfather was hesitant at first because he thought that Coyote Thunder would be hurt if he left and went on his search for purity. Grandfather evasively told Coyote Thunder that the old one had helped him with his secret Vision, and he would discuss it more with him when he had fully thought it through. Coyote Thunder looked at Grandfather for a long moment and said, "There is no time for thinking; now is the time for action. You must complete what I had begun so many years ago. The people will be safe in the sacred canyon, and you will be free to come and go as you please. There life will be easy for us, and we will be well protected. What you seek is far more important. If by chance we should die in your absence, it will not be in vain, for what you seek the world must know." Without waiting for a reply Coyote Thunder walked away, leaving Grandfather to his thoughts and overwhelming astonishment.

Grandfather helped pack and move the little camp to the sacred canyon and stayed there until the camp was rebuilt and the foodstores for the winter were full. He hesitated from discussing anything about his quest with anyone. As far as he was concerned, he would begin his journey sometime in the spring. That way he could at least be a help to his people if the winter got bad. Then, one night while he sat with Coyote Thunder by the fire, Coyote Thunder told him that he was no longer needed here. He said, "Your work here is done for a while. The people will do well, for the Earth has told me of a mild winter. You must not delay your first quest until the spring, for to hesitate now is to postpone the Vision. You will wander through the next thirteen moons, and with each journey you will find many answers, but it is within the next moon that you will understand the purity you seek. I have held council with the spirits, and this is what they have told me."

Grandfather felt a great sense of relief wash over him, for his fears were now vanquished. He had worried about leaving, but now Coyote Thunder had told him to go, almost demanded that he leave right away. He could feel the intensity in Coyote Thunder's voice, an intensity that almost bordered on desperation. It was as if it were an answer to Coyote Thunder's dreams, as if he, too, would accompany Grandfather. So, too, was it a relief that most of what he would learn would be within the next moon. He knew that he would be back to camp frequently and could still be a help. He decided to leave the next morning, before first light. That way he would not have to discuss his search with anyone, for he didn't even know where he was going. However, he could feel now the powerful spiritual beckoning deep inside of him, and he knew that he would find the truth.

2

Religion Revealed

Grandfather had wandered for several days, not sure yet as to where he was going or when he would be able to return to his people. His excitement over finally getting his search for purity underway had given in to feelings of confusion. The spiritual beckoning was still strong, but it had been leading him deep into White man's lands, and his journey had now been slowed to almost a crawl. He had to become hypervigilant so as not to be detected by the Whites. Every move had to be planned, every action thoroughly thought through. Eventually he had to go to full scout tactics, not only making his camps invisible, but also traveling at night and sleeping during the day. Even his night travel had to be restricted to the very late evening and wee hours of the morning, when most people would be asleep. He was forced at this time to eat only plants, in that hunting was out of the question.

He did not like coming anywhere near the White man, for he had encountered nothing but trouble whenever he came close to their camps. Though he always remained unseen, he

still felt dirty and disgusted over what he saw. Nothing that
the White man did made any sense. All the Whites seemed
to want to do was to destroy the land and kill the Indians.
They were aliens to the earth, a disease, which Grandfather
feared would spread to him. He began to seriously question
the wisdom of his spiritual guidance. He could not understand
what would be learned from the White man. Certainly their
religions interested him, but he had been hoping to study
religion with the Hopi people or with the people of the
jungles far to the south. He never anticipated being so close
to the White death, nor could he imagine what he could ever
learn from them that would be of any value.

As he moved deeper into the White man's lands, fear
bordering on terror began to obscure his Inner Vision. The
farther he went, the more he felt out of touch with his spirit.
It seemed to him that the consciousness of the White man
was affecting and poisoning his mind and spirit. Many times
he desperately wanted to retreat to the safety of his people,
but each time the thought of running came over him, his
spiritual drive forced him onward. Deep inside him there
was a tremendous battle going on. It took all of his power
just to keep going. Fear became his constant enemy and the
hypervigilance exhausted his senses. Everywhere he looked
were the signs of the White man. Farms gave way to hamlets
and towns, wilderness became civilized and trodden. Livestock replaced most wild animals, and even the air had the
stench of the White man.

Grandfather also feared getting a sickness from the White
man. He had heard many stories about Native Peoples dying
from the many diseases the White man brought with him.
He knew that his people were rarely sick, and if so, never
for very long. The White man always seemed sick, afflicted
with all manner of ailments that his people never knew. He
was afraid to drink any water, so he drank rarely and only
from a spring. He feared walking on the land, for even that
felt sick and defiled. He learned quickly that all outhouses
should be avoided. Here the stench of rotting human waste
was more than he could bare. He would grow physically

sick and break into a panicked run anytime he inadvertently walked downwind of one as he moved through the night. The stench of White man as well as the stench of livestock seemed to become imbedded in his very flesh. Even the earth smelled badly at times.

The farm fields and small scattered hamlets now gave way to larger developed areas and towns. It was on the edge of one of these towns that Grandfather's spirit called to him to stop his journey, set camp, and rest. Resting was rather difficult, for he felt like an alien in this place. His only place of refuge and escape was countless miles away in the misty mountains barely visible from where he camped. Though his camp was in a very secluded and rugged area, invisible to most, he still felt very uneasy. Only at night could he have a small campfire, which had to be built in a deep hole so the light would not be seen. Wood had to be small and dry so there would be no smoke. And food had to be collected in such a way that no one would notice. His little camp became an island of reprieve in a sea of ,White man's wilderness. Sleep was fitful at best, sometimes nearly impossible, for as soon as Grandfather heard any distant noise that was not natural, he would be jolted awake, senses straining to identify any possible danger.

It was during the second day in his camp, while in a deep sleep, that the spirit of the old woman appeared in Grandfather's dream. It was just the image of her face, calling to him to awaken. Grandfather listened intently as the old woman spoke, saying, "You have now arrived at the dawn of your quest for purity. It is here in the alien world of the White man that you will begin to find what you are looking for. I know you worry that you will be found, but there is no other way to lead you to what you must begin to understand. It is here, hidden in the beliefs of the White man, that you will understand the essence of modern religion. Go then, using all your skill to avoid detection, to the white building with the crossed sticks high above. Observe carefully, listen, look beyond the facade, and understand what you witness."

Grandfather awoke slowly to the lingering departure of the old woman's spirit. Even with his eyes fully open, he could still vaguely make out her image, now pointing in the direction of the white building. There was no doubt in his mind that he had to go to this place immediately. Without hesitation, he further concealed his camp and tracks and departed in the direction that the old woman had pointed.

Traveling in the day was a nightmare. It required a pace far slower and more careful than he had yet experienced. His senses were on full alert, and his hypervigilance was exhausting. He knew now that he had no other choice but to follow the old woman's instructions without fail. This was an important part of his Vision and there could be no other way. As always, he had to seek his Vision or die, for there could be no life without a living Vision.

Finally he arrived at the white structure with the crossed sticks of which the old woman spoke. He knew without a doubt that this was a church, for he had so often heard Coyote Thunder speak of these places. Fortunately, the church was located in the least-populated portion of town and surrounded on three sides by thick underbrush and heavy forest. As Grandfather arrived, the sun was well into its set, but the church was deserted. There was no evidence of anyone about. As darkness came over the land, Grandfather crawled to the edge of the forest and checked the footprints around its edge. It appeared to him that many people had been there at one time, but the tracks were a few days old. No fresher tracks could be seen. The building remained dark inside. Grandfather wondered if there was another place where the people worshiped, prayed, and sought the things of the spirit.

Late into the night, Grandfather crept up to the large windows and peered inside. He could see nothing at all. He could barely make out shadowy images of furniture, but nothing more. Instead of returning to his camp, he decided to stay put. The journey to and from his camp would be treacherous at best. Instead, he built a small temporary camp deep in the thickest portion of forest next to the church. He took great care in selecting the site, making sure it was far

from trails where people could walk. It took him the better
part of the night to finish the camp, though he fell to sleep
not in his shelter, but next to it, such was his exhaustion in
body and emotion. His nerves were frazzled being so deep
into the White man's territory.

He was abruptly awakened in the early morning by a
hammering sound, so alien to the sound of pounding rock
that he was familiar with. He slipped to the edge of the forest
and crawled the few remaining feet so he could get a full view
of the origin of the sound. There by the front of the church
were two men. One man was hammering on the steps of the
church, and the other was holding a board. They appeared to
be repairing something. Within an hour the work was complete, and the men departed, without going into the church.
Grandfather decided to stay put to see if others would show
up. He lay all day and through most of the night, but no one
came to the church. It looked deserted and relatively abandoned. Again there was no light in the church at night. He
repeated his vigil for several more days, but still no one came.
At times people passed by, but no one entered the church.

Finally, late one afternoon, several people arrived at the
church and met outside. They carried no tools but seemed to
be waiting for the arrival of something or someone. Finally
an elderly man arrived, followed by the commotion of chatter
and handshaking, and the small group went inside. After a
long wait Grandfather approached the windows of the church,
using the deep evening shadows to disguise his movements.
A light burned in the far corner of the church, and people sat
in a small semicircle around the old man. The old one had
removed his coat, and Grandfather could see the white collar
which marked him as the priest or minister. Grandfather
again remembered Coyote Thunder mentioning the clothing
and customs of the White man's religious leaders. The people
sat in an attitude of prayer. Every so often one would stand
and talk out loud, eyes closed, and face lifted toward the
rafters of the church. Then, in a short period of time, they
all sang a song and departed the church. Everything was
returned to darkened silence.

Back in camp, Grandfather reflected on the things he had witnessed. He could not understand why the church remained abandoned most of the time. In his culture, every moment of every day was dedicated to the Creator and seeking the things of the spirit. There was not an action that his people undertook that did not have deep spiritual implications. Each day the people met for prayer, each day everyone dedicated a portion of his time to the "sacred silence." It was very obvious to Grandfather that the White man's church was not the center of his daily life, as it was to the Native Peoples. Grandfather could not understand why anyone would want to worship and pray in a building, cut off from the power and life-giving forces of nature. After all, nature was the physical manifestation of the Creator's love, the holiest temple known to man. Grandfather remained baffled.

Again Grandfather returned to the church before dawn on the following day. He lay for hours in the brush, watching the deserted church. Finally several people began to gather in front of the church, along with the holy man. They chatted for a while as more people began to arrive. This time there were many more, children included. The holy man unlocked the church, which shocked Grandfather. He could not believe that the church had to be locked, nor could he guess for what reason. More and more people began to arrive, most entering the church immediately in a hurried manner. Few behaved as if they were entering a holy temple, and many of the children did not look as if they wanted to go inside. Most appeared to want to play outside instead. Finally the doors were closed, and singing began to emerge from inside. Yet it was not a joyous singing, it sounded more like a chore. Grandfather could feel that the song was just sung for the sake of the singing and not for the reality of spiritual truth.

Very carefully Grandfather crept to the edge of the church. There was no one about, but it was full daylight and there was no place to hide. He cautiously approached the window and looked inside. The holy man spoke in a loud voice. Some people listened attentively, but most just sat with blank looks on their faces, appearing totally oblivious to what was being said. Children were restless in their seats, and some people were dozing. There was a long talk from the holy man, followed by an equally long and drawn-out prayer, when everyone stood in bowed silence. Immediately after the prayer the doors were flung open and people began to go outside. Grandfather slipped back into the underbrush like a shadow. He felt so confused over what he had witnessed. For a place of spirit, this place seemed to have no spirit. The people seemed to be far away from this place in their hearts and minds. Only the old ones, those that were close to death, seemed the least bit interested.

Grandfather watched most of the people hurry from the church, as if they had other more important things to do. Only a few stayed outside talking, even then only briefly before they, too, departed. Again the church remained silent for most of the day. Grandfather lay in wait to see what else might transpire on this obviously holy day. Nothing happened until near sunset, when the church was again opened to people. However, this was a small group, barely half the number that had come in the morning. When the meeting was over, they all left with greater haste than they had in the morning. Again, all was silent, the church dark and deserted. Grandfather came to the church every day and evening for the next several days, but six suns passed before the worship process was repeated. Grandfather was shocked at the way the White man sought the wisdom of the spirit. Could it be that the White man set aside only one day in seven suns to worship, pray, and seek the things of the spirit?

Grandfather returned to his first camp, far away from the church. It was obvious that nothing more could be learned there. In a way, he began to feel sorry for the people he saw. They looked so bored and full of some unfounded sorrow. He wondered what he could learn from what he saw in that church. Surely this could not be the way of all White culture. He then remembered what Coyote Thunder had said of the White man, that this was the way they worshiped. There was not much more beyond the church. Coyote Thunder had said that the White man's religion was more something they had to do, rather than wanted to do. Many were forced to church because they worried what others might think, or because they believed that this was the only way to come close to their God. Grandfather's mind swooned with all manner of thoughts of the church and all Coyote Thunder had told him. The more he thought, the more confused he became. Finally he gave in to a much needed sleep, determined to get back to the sanctuary of wilderness the next day.

While in a deep sleep, Grandfather was propelled into a lucid dream, where he was actually standing in the very church he had observed. He could not only hear but also understand the words the holy man spoke. He could hear and understand the prayers of the people as well as their songs. He saw all things so clearly that they became real. He observed the whole sermon and all the actions and reactions of the people, then, just as suddenly as it came to him, it was all gone, and without awakening he fell back into a deep sleep. The next morning he awoke refreshed, but with the dream still foremost on his mind. He searched it for meanings, but none were apparent. This troubled him, for he had not a clue as to what he had to learn from it. He knew this kind of dream was important, but the importance would not reveal itself. It only became more vague and complicated as he tried to sort it all out.

He was so preoccupied with the dream that he did nothing else all day, not even entertain the thought of leaving his camp, like he had decided the previous night. Tired of sitting and thinking for so long, he unconsciously began to wander the landscape, caring little about where he was going or how long he would be gone. The interpretation of the dream was the single most important thing on his mind. He was shocked to find that his wanderings had taken him to the back woods of the church, a place where he had not yet been. So unconscious had been his walk that finding himself there actually confused and shocked him. He began to realize very quickly that his arrival there was not by chance, but guided by some outside spiritual force. Without question he sat down and waited, but for what he did not know.

As the sun gave way to darkness, he again slipped into deep thought about last night's dream. No longer was he consumed with just waiting, but still no clear answers came to him. It was then that he clearly heard the old woman's voice saying, "Look beyond the apparent. Seek the wisdom of the whole." As soon as Grandfather got over the sudden shock of the voice, he began to understand what the old woman was asking him to do. He had been far too busy deciphering the details and failed to see and understand what the overall experience wanted to convey to him. He then focused his attention not on the congregation, the sermon, the prayers, or the song, but the overall reason for them to be in the church. The answer hit him like a plunge into cold water. The answer was so obvious that he could not understand why he had overlooked it in the first place.

He immediately realized why all these people were gathered in the church. It was simply to worship the Creator and to give thanks. However, it seemed to him that most prayers and sermons were actually asking things of the Creator, not only on a personal plane but also on a community level. There was very little thanksgiving, and no spiritual teachings as far as he could see. He wondered if the White man used only this small portion of time every seven suns to give thanks and to ask the Creator for help. What of the many other days? Is the Creator set aside and nearly forgotten? And what of the deeper spiritual teachings and quests? Is there no time set aside in the world of the White man for these things? To his people, the quest for spiritual ability was foremost, along with the constant sense of thanksgiving and prayer. Then and only then came the worship, but all were continuous and equal. All the White man seemed to want was the divine intervention of the Creator.

Most of all, Grandfather could not understand the way the White man worshiped. It was so alien to his thinking that anyone would want to be removed from the cathedrals of nature. For only in wilderness, that which is built by the Creator, can man ever hope to draw near to God. Why is it then that the White man seeks to hide himself in structures built by his hands, that ultimately keep him from the life-giving forces of the earth? Has the White man something to hide, or does he fear what God has made? Coyote Thunder many times had talked of a man named Jesus, who used the gardens, the mountains, and the wilderness as a place to worship. Could these White men be praying to the same God that had taught Jesus this kind of simplicity? Where now is the simplicity of Jesus, he thought, for all he could see in the White man's worship was complication.

The more Grandfather thought, the more confusing the religion of the White man became. Even this holy man became a paradox in Grandfather's mind. Grandfather had been taught that the only way to the Creator was through the heart. Each person must approach the Creator alone. Each person must seek the wisdom of the spirit alone. To Grandfather, there was no church, no leader, only his heart and the voice of the Creator, which spoke to him through Inner Vision. Why then must there be this holy man who seemed to dictate to the people what they should believe? The elders and medicine people of Grandfather's tribe did not dictate but suggested and advised. What made this White man's holy man so special that he could know and dictate exactly how each person must seek the Creator? This seemed so absurd to Grandfather.

Grandfather then began to wonder what nature and the earth would say of the White man's religion. He now remembered Coyote Thunder's teaching so vividly. Coyote Thunder had told him after learning of spiritual things, take them to the wilderness. If these teachings work there and work for everyone, then they are universal truths. Grandfather could not see the White man's philosophy and religion working for all people. So, too, did he wonder what would happen if all of the cherished books and teachings of the White man were taken away. Could the White man then understand that which is spoken on the wings of the wind? Could he understand that which is conveyed through the tongues of the earth? To Grandfather, the White man knew only the language of man, and not the tongues of nature and spirit. Grandfather felt that if it could not be articulated, then it could not be understood by the White man. He was just too far removed from the earth, like his church, to understand.

It was late by the time Grandfather arrived back in his little camp. He felt this was all he needed to know for now and would leave at first light for his people. He had gathered so many questions about the White man that he needed the wisdom of Coyote Thunder to sort it out. He was not asleep long when the old woman again appeared to him in a dream and said, "You will leave this place with the rising of the sun, but you need not seek the wisdom of the elders. They cannot help you, for you have all you need to know. They will not fully understand. You have gone beyond that which they will understand, for they have not witnessed the things you have observed. Again, I ask you to look away from the confusing details and understand the whole." With those words she was gone again, leaving Grandfather to his sleep.

As dawn sky came, Grandfather was on his way back to the sanctuary of the distant mountains. As he cautiously traveled, he ruminated over the words of the old woman. What was he missing in the larger picture? What else was there to understand? What could he have possibly missed? Then he remembered the prayers of the congregation, and what was missing became obvious. Most, if not all, of the prayers were for things of the flesh. It was painfully apparent that the White man cherished the flesh more than the riches of the spirit. The way the White man lived, the way he acted, the way he worked, and even the way he worshiped was for the satisfaction of the flesh. Grandfather wondered if the only god the White man worshiped was the god of the flesh, for that is where his focus seemed to exist. In fact during all the time Grandfather spent by the church, this supposedly sacred place, he did not sense the deep rapture of spirit. All he felt was a sense of flesh. There was no sense of spirit in the congregation, just flesh and the riches of the flesh. People had been more interested in each other than in God. Fully disgusted now, he walked on, concentrating no more on the shallowness of these people.

Several days later Grandfather finally arrived at the mountains, and within the next rise of the sun, he was far away from the White man's domain. Once in the sanctuary of the mountains, he felt safe and at home. The spirit of wilderness began to replace the destruction of civilization. Creation seemed to be in song for his return. Each entity of the land seemed to welcome him, and he could feel the spirits of the unseen and eternal walking with him. This was his grand cathedral, closest to God. No building of the White man could attain this splendor, this spiritual intensity. Here was the truth, spoken by the winds, whispered by the grasses, and written across the sky. Here the heart was the guide and the voice of the Creator could be felt within. Here there was no inner or outer dimension, just spirit, and the flesh was set aside. Here the rapture worked for everyone and everything. It was truth.

Not long after entering the mountains, Grandfather began to understand the greater lessons of what he had witnessed. The White man's ways were so complicated, so corrupted, so much talk and flesh. Here in the wilderness was simplicity, purity, and truth. Here he was at home with his brothers and sisters, and with his mother the earth. So, too, was he in the world of spirit, for here he walked a duality that the White men could never know, as long as they worshiped and prayed only for flesh. Only when the White man set aside the quests of the flesh and sought spiritual enlightenment could he know the duality of self. That is what was missing from the White man's ways, spiritual enlightenment, enlightenment that cannot be taught, but understood only through the heart. Now Grandfather could fully understand the difference between worship and spirituality. White man worships and prays only for flesh and does not seek spiritual enlightenment.

3

Of Belief and Purity

Grandfather had been wandering in the mountains for several days, happy to finally be free of the White man's civilization and his polluted lands and lopsided religions. As he wandered, his mind began to clear and he began to walk once again the duality of flesh and spirit. Truly, the Earth was the physical manifestation of the Creator's love, a gift to be cherished and taken care of. He could not understand why the White man chose to defile the gift and remove himself from its power whenever possible. The more Grandfather thought about White men, the less he understood their ways. There was no sense in what they did. They seemed to live just to complicate, destroy, and gather unto themselves the things of the flesh. Why could White men not see the wisdom and purity of the wilderness? Was it because they had been removed for so long from its power and forgotten what it was like, or did they just lack true belief?

Although he tried, Grandfather could not free himself from the swirl of questions that flooded his mind. What especially concerned him were the questions as to why White men

41

removed themselves from the Earth, and why their religions were based almost entirely on worship and praying for things of the flesh. With these paramount questions foremost in his mind, Grandfather decided not to go back to his people right away, but to wander and let his spirit guide him. He wanted to gain some insight into these questions before approaching Coyote Thunder and the elders with what he had discovered. Right now he could not fully understand enough even to ask the right questions, far less try to convey what he had witnessed. He needed time, pure time, spiritual time, to work things through.

His southward wanderings through the mountains eventually led him to an old and abandoned kiva, one he had visited many years before with Coyote Thunder. As soon as he saw it, he knew that he had to stay in this sacred place for a while. Before entering the general area he knelt and prayed, asking the spirits for permission to be here and to guide him on his quest. He dared not enter the sacred kiva, for it was not part of his religion. Yet he held it sacred because it was sacred to others, as the church was sacred to others, and thus it demanded respect. Grandfather knew he could not condemn anyone for their beliefs, for each must worship as his heart dictated. It was not for Grandfather to decide which was right or wrong, for each must decide his own path. Grandfather had been taught that there are many paths that lead to the path of purity and ultimately to the Creator. Each person, right or wrong, must follow his own path, no matter how confusing or complicated it may appear.

Grandfather prepared camp well outside the kiva area. As the sun set, all the work was finished, and Grandfather fell into a lucid daydream, though fully awake. He imagined the ancient drummers and dancers that once worshiped here. He could feel the prayers and hear the chants. He could see the images of spirits past dancing in the firelight. He sensed a certain closeness with these people, for their beliefs were similar to those common to his people. Suddenly he began to see all of this through the questioning eyes of the White man. He felt a certain sense of awe and mystery, but so, too, with the White man's mind he felt a great resentment, condemnation, and sense of it all being wrong. He began to look at the worship as a form of pagan idolatry. The feeling hit him so suddenly and so powerfully that he had to physically stand up to unlock the hold of the daydream. He was shocked at the things he had felt and thought.

The reason for this waking vision became painfully apparent. There was no need for prolonged analysis. By perceiving like a White man for just an instant, he could feel what they felt. Surely they also must feel the same way about Grandfather's form of worship. They looked upon these rituals the same way Grandfather had looked upon theirs. It was disturbingly obvious that everyone believed their way was right, no matter how complicated or distorted. Each person felt his or her religion was the only way to the Creator, and the only way that worked. Grandfather decided that it was insane to judge another philosophy or religion, but accord each the right to follow his or her own path. He then began to feel a little foolish in condemning the White man's church, even though this condemnation came through his own confusion.

Grandfather could feel himself approaching the verge of a greater understanding, though he knew he had not yet arrived at that point. As he pondered, he began to focus on the word *worked*. For a religion or philosophy to work, it must be proven first in the temples of creation and then be proven to work for everyone. *Work* also meant there had to be reproducible miraculous results. At this point in his thoughts, he began to unconsciously back away and look at the overall landscapes of religion and philosophy. Like the winged of the East, he removed himself from the prejudice of his own mind and looked down from his lofty flight. He saw all the religions, philosophies, and beliefs of the world, each proclaiming their righteousness, but none working for everyone and certainly not in the purity of creation. He then realized that there must be a common thread that binds all of these together in some divine way, a dynamic and pure connection, a reality common to the whole. But what was that reality?

All of this time, as far back as he could remember, Grandfather saw only the differences in the religions and philosophies, and judged them on those differences as compared to his own. Now his perception had made a dramatic change. Instead of seeking the differences, he had to search for the similarities, that which ultimately bound all together. So much time had been wasted on prejudicial comparisons and righteousness, but now he could see clearly and understand as a child. If he could find the common thread, the pure truth, embedded in each philosophy and religion, then there could be no right or wrong. Then each would hold the truth in some way, no matter how polluted by the dogmas, customs, traditions, and ceremonies of man. It was paramount that this basic truth or truths be found. This then was his Vision, his quest, and his purpose.

Armed now with this new understanding and insight, Grandfather knew what he had to do. He had to look at all religions, philosophies, and beliefs purely and without prejudice. He had to learn the ways of people, then search each for that common truth, that ultimate purity. Once he understood that purity, he might then know what caused each to become different. Right now he understood one important concept; there was no right or wrong, just simple differences. For some reason, this avalanche of understanding cleansed his spirit, banished the prisons of prejudice, and revealed to him a very definite path. An overwhelming excitement and anticipation filled him, transcending the flesh and enrapturing his very spirit. All of his visions and dreams finally could be understood. It was at this point of understanding that Grandfather had to arrive before he could continue with his work.

Along with this tremendous enlightenment came an extreme physical, mental, and emotional fatigue. It was as if the entire exhausting journey to the White man's world had finally caught up to him, and he had to go to his shelter and sleep. There would be time enough tomorrow for his search to begin. Right now he needed sleep very badly; otherwise, the line between true enlightenment and hallucination would be crossed. Grandfather knew from past experience that extreme fatigue produced distortion. He knew when to let go of the search. Now he knew he had to give in to the exhaustion, otherwise pay the penalty of defiling the truth. No sooner did he close his eyes than he was fast asleep.

He awoke to what he thought was the faint light of dawn, only to discover that he was looking through a small hole high above him. At first he did not know where he was, but upon close inspection he found himself, to his shock, in the heart of the kiva. He had no idea as to how he got there; possibly he walked in his sleep. But there was no ladder from the hole to the ground he sat upon. He was perplexed to say the least. He sat for a long time before he attempted to stand, not only to come fully awake, but also to try to figure out how he got into this place. As he sat, he looked at the faint light hitting the ground. There were no tracks other than the outline of where he had lain. This further confused him. He soon resigned himself to the fact that he had gotten into the kiva somehow, and right now there was nothing he could do about it. Certainly there was no way out. In a way he was imprisoned, for the entrance was higher than he could possibly jump.

As Grandfather sat contemplating his predicament and possible route of escape, he began to hear faint voices or chanting, the source of which he could not determine. He gazed around the kiva trying to determine their origin, but the light did not reach beyond the faint illumination of the ground before him. His head seemed to spin in a daze of images as the voices and chanting mixed, intensified, and surrounded him. They intensified to an almost deafening level, then abruptly stopped. The silence that followed was almost as deafening. The silence lasted for what seemed to be an eternity, and then suddenly a faint image began to appear at the far wall of the kiva. Grandfather could hear his breathing and heartbeat in the silence of his anticipation. At first appearance the image seemed to be the old woman, but soon the image shifted like the windblown surface of a once quiet pond, now only to reveal itself as an old and weatherbeaten man.

As Grandfather gazed at the apparition, he could feel the wind and hear the sound of fluttering wings, like an owl passing close overhead. The old one whispered Grandfather's name, sending Grandfather into a bolt upright position. The old one spoke softly, saying, "I have waited for you to come. I once thought that your Great-grandfather would be the one, but choice and necessity led him elsewhere. Now you fulfil his destiny." Silence returned to the kiva as the old man paused. Grandfather wondered how the old man had known his name or the name of his Great-grandfather. This man, or spirit, was dressed in the clothing of people who long ago passed away, even long before Coyote Thunder's Great-grandfather was born. It was rare that Grandfather was startled by spiritual encounters, but this one was more than startling.

As Grandfather's mind returned to the silence of the kiva, the old man spoke again, saying, "You have come to the edge of a great wisdom, child, and now you must continue your journey. You see, long ago, when people lived close to the earth, there was but one truth, one way. But as man moved away from the earth, he found it difficult to get back to the reality of spirit. He devised new and different ways to reach the spiritual truths and purity of duality. Man began to live more in the flesh than in the spirit. Soon he began to live wholly in the flesh and the journey back to spirit became nearly impossible. Man then felt the loss, and his spirit slept. He tried many things to awaken his spirit, but at best they were ineffective. The physical mind began to overpower and dominate the spiritual mind. Soon the spiritual mind was imprisoned by thought and flesh. The voice of the heart was stilled."

After a long silence the old man continued, saying, "Man then devised ways to try to awaken his spiritual body and mind. He knew that he first must unlock the prison of his flesh and his physical mind in order to set his spirit free. He began to develop complicated ritual, custom, ceremony, and tradition. Chants, songs, singing, prayers, and all manner of other techniques to quiet the physical mind and placate the flesh were devised, but to no avail. Man's logical mind was still dominant and imprisoning. At best, the spiritual realities remained distorted and brief. There was a frustration which began to grow, for man could no longer reach the spirit. The complications, distortions, and frustrations further drove man from the spiritual path and deeper into the flesh."

Silence again permeated the kiva as the old man allowed Grandfather to digest what he had told him. He continued, "It is then man's mind and flesh which first drove him from the spiritual duality, and now man tries to devise things derived from that same mind and flesh to get him back. This cannot be done, for the logical mind only succeeds to complicate and further imprison with all its distorted ritual. Modern man is locked in a cycle which only further removes him from the wisdom and purity of spiritual existence. What remains is for man to throw away all the distorted complications and get back to the purity. The only way this can and will be done is to quiet the physical mind and flesh. It is through this quiet mind, this pure mind, that mankind will again be able to walk the duality. It is then and only then that the physical and spiritual mind and body will be fused into a pure oneness."

"But how is this done?" Grandfather asked the old man.

"You already know, child," said the old man. "You have been to that place before, and even now you live that wisdom most of the time, especially when you are alone in the cathedrals of creation. The problem you face is to first define this wisdom, and then learn to live it in the company of others. It is then that you can pass it to the white coyote of your Vision."

"But I do not know how to reach the purity of the spiritual mind," said Grandfather.

"Yes you do, and you do it well," said the old man. "Your only problem is that you do not know what you do, you just do it naturally. Now look at me." With that the old man's image intensified, then appeared to be submerged or behind a wall of clear still water, though still very vivid. "This is me through your spiritual mind as seen through your spiritual eyes," said the old man. Then the image began to distort as ripples began to appear on the surface of the waters. Now the surface stirred with waves, ripples, and the image was gone. From somewhere in the waters the old man's voice said, "And this is your spiritual mind disturbed with thoughts. That is the wisdom you now must seek and identify." With those words the old one was gone.

The kiva fell dark, except for the faint light on the floor that shafted through its opening. Grandfather began to think hard about what the old man with no name had told him. The old one had certainly been right. Somewhere inside, Grandfather had known all along what the old man had told him, but it took this encounter for all to become clear. Grandfather knew that the physical mind imprisoned and obscured spiritual thoughts, and the more man existed in the flesh of body and mind, the more the spirit was imprisoned. He also knew that it was difficult at times to attain that spiritual clarity in the company of others, even with the highly spiritually oriented people of his family. With the White man it was nearly impossible. What he had to do now was to try to find a way that brought forth the spiritual mind under any condition or distraction. Yet he was not sure how this could be achieved.

Grandfather began to think about the kiva, the Vision Quest, the sweatlodge, and the temples, churches, and worship areas of man. Were these not a way of quieting the physical mind so the spiritual mind could awaken and function? So, too, with the countless customs, ceremonies, dogmas, and traditions of religion, for these were also a way to set aside the flesh and open the world of spirit. But to be pure and free, man had to transcend these things and arrive at the spirit consciousness without using all of these complicated crutches. Looking at it coldly and from afar, Grandfather wondered if the cathedrals of creation were also a crutch. They were certainly a far better crutch, a natural and pure crutch, but nonetheless a crutch. He knew there must be a simplicity in the approach, free of all crutches, for it is the crutches that mark the differences in religions and beliefs.

Grandfather then realized it is the emerging of the pure and spiritual mind that becomes a common thread, a common truth, that binds all religions and philosophies together.

Grandfather had found the first common thread, that of spiritual awakening and purity. But, he thought, what is the second common thread, the third, and beyond? As Grandfather searched his heart in the silence of the kiva, the word suddenly shifted into his consciousness—the word was *belief*. He was so overwhelmed by the intensity of the experience he stood up and let out an eagle's scream. The scream ended and Grandfather realized he was standing outside his shelter facing the rising sun. He was fully awake and it had all been one tremendous dream, but a dream of truth. He would not allow himself the luxury of trying to figure out how he got from the kiva to where he now stood, or if he had been in the kiva at all. He would not even go to the kiva and look inside for tracks. He did not care how he arrived at these truths, for he now possessed the wisdom, and it felt so good. Now he had to turn the wisdom into rock-solid answers.

Grandfather now had two areas that he must explore, that of pure mind or spiritual mind, and that of belief. There was no doubt in his conscious mind that these things were truly a basis of many philosophies and religions; however, these same philosophies and religions were now distorted by the many doctrines and rituals invented. Grandfather knew his search must now discover how to arrive at this pure mind at will, and how to attain that unwavering faith, that pure belief. For it is through the pure mind that all spiritual communications must come, and it is through belief that we empower those communications. What then is that vehicle, that purity? Grandfather knew that it must lie somewhere in the wisdom of the "Sacred Silence." But the Sacred Silence was known only to his people. He wondered if it could also be known by others and if it could be understood by others.

4

Religion Transcended

Grandfather departed the sacred kiva that day and continued on his journey. He had not decided whether to go back to his people or not or if he just wanted to allow the journey itself to take him where he needed to go. His main concern now was to look into the wisdom of the Sacred Silence and see if in fact other religions and philosophies possessed similar knowledge. As Grandfather wandered, he could again feel a tremendous spiritual draw that began to lead him to the outer edge of the mountain wilderness. He looked down on the distant plains that stretched before him with their various planted fields, fence rows, and grazing cattle that now replaced the buffalo. So, too, did he see a curious straight ribbon of roadway, but he was too high up and too far away to make out exactly its purpose. He gazed at it for a long time, for never before, even in the strange world of the White man, did he encounter such a thing.

In the distance Grandfather heard a prolonged wailing sound, and on the horizon he saw billowing smoke. As he watched, the smoke came closer and closer, moving quickly along the roadway. The wailing sounded again, now closer and clearer. Along with the wailing came a panting and hissing, the likes of which he never before heard. Held in awe by this terrifying sight, he began to make out what looked like some kind of vehicle, long and segmented, like a snake. It was then he realized that what he was seeing was a railroad train. He had heard Coyote Thunder tell stories of this machine, but Grandfather never before had seen one. It was more horrifying and sickening than he could ever imagine. It was on this vehicle that the White man moved from ocean to ocean without bother, in a blinding mechanical rush of encapsulation. At that moment he was glad Coyote Thunder had hidden his people for all of these years away from the insanity of the White man.

Grandfather knew deep inside that it was not to the railroad that the spirit guided him, but along the outer range of the mountains. Now the spiritual draw was more powerful and with greater purpose. The spirit would not allow him to relax or rest for very long. His journey eventually took him down the mountains and into the lower elevations, finally coming to the thick forests of the foothills. Here he had to take more care in his travels, for this was the kind of land in which "those who lust for gold" would be found. He wandered through the day and night and to the next dawn without sleep, such was the demanding pull of his Inner Vision. Finally his trail halted at the edge of a small clearing, and nestled there was a small cabin. Grandfather carefully approached, and once in sight of the front porch, he saw an old white man sitting in a rocking chair, apparently watching the rising sun.

Grandfather watched him for quite some time. His actions were so atypical to that of a normal White man. Possibly his great age had opened his eyes and heart to the things around him. Grandfather could sense that there was no danger here, for the tracks foretold that this old man lived alone. Grandfather stepped to the edge of the clearing to see if the old man would notice. The old man glanced toward Grandfather, shook his head in disbelief, then a broad smile crept over his face. He lifted his hand in a hesitant wave, and Grandfather returned the gesture. The man called and motioned Grandfather over to the house. At first Grandfather didn't want to go, but the spiritual urging hit him and he had no choice. Though he could detect no immediate danger, his heart pounded in his chest as he walked to the house.

To Grandfather's surprise, the old man spoke to him in his own tongue, broken and labored, but understandable. The old man was very warm and hospitable, offering Grandfather some herbal tea while chatting away about the beauty of the mountains. It was obvious that the old man needed the company, and Grandfather was more than eager to oblige. So, too, did Grandfather need the company, a good rest, and possibly more knowledge of this old man and why he was here. Almost from the start, Grandfather knew that this old one would answer many of the questions he had of the White man's ways. Though at first the conversation was a little restricted and formal, by high sun they were both laughing at each other's jokes and swapping stories of their wanderings. This old White man was more like one of Grandfather's people than his White counterparts. This man was special.

Grandfather spent the next several days with the old one. The old man, called Torrence, became very instrumental in helping Grandfather to understand the ways of the White man, and subsequently the various religions and beliefs of the White man. Grandfather was also delighted to find that Torrence no longer believed in the ways of the White man, either on a physical level or in the wisdom of the spirit. Instead, he followed another philosophy, and that was the major reason why he now lived alone in the wilderness. The White world no longer understood him, nor did they speak a common tongue. He had become a social outcast, more by choice than by design. Torrence told Grandfather that he was a student of the earth and the philosophy of life, much like Grandfather. So, too, was Torrence a searcher of truth.

Grandfather was amazed at how much Torrence knew. He was also very curious as to what drove Torrence away from

White society to the path he was now on. During the last day they were together, Grandfather asked Torrence what happened in his life to change his beliefs. Torrence related a delightful story of his rebirth. Apparently he had worked for a time, years earlier, as a line foreman on a small railroad building project. Under his leadership were a handful of foreigners that were generally treated like beasts of burden by the Whites. Torrence began to love these people and their philosophy and treated them as he would treat himself, much to the anger of his superiors. He grew particularly friendly with an old man that was several years his senior. This man, called Zee, was the one who led Torrence from the beliefs of the White man to a richer philosophy. His friendship with Zee was also directly responsible for his early retirement and subsequent pilgrimage to the wilderness.

Torrence told Grandfather that Zee was still alive and healthy, living only a few miles from his cabin, in a small place of his own. Zee was not of the White nor the native culture, but from lands far off. Torrence considered Zee a sort of medicine man, very knowledgeable in the ways of many cultures and philosophies. Zee's peers considered him a sage and went to him often for healing herbs and advice. Zee was also friendly to many of the local native medicine men and women, and well respected. As Grandfather listened to the many stories about Zee, it became a necessity to meet him and possibly share medicine. Grandfather was truly amazed and excited about the prospects of meeting this man called Zee. There was no doubt in Grandfather's mind that this was why the spirit had led him to Torrence in the first place. That evening Torrence and Grandfather prepared to leave to visit Zee. They were gone with the rising sun.

Zee's cabin was remarkably tidy and strange, like nothing Grandfather had ever seen before. The gardens surrounding it were neat and well kept, showing tremendous love for the earth. His home was also a garden, decorated here and there with chimes, strange tapestry, candles, and many other religious artifacts. Zee was very old, wrinkled, and gray, but his energy seemed limitless, his laughter contagious. In many of the things he did, there was a touch of childlike wonder and enthusiasm. Zee's wisdom went far beyond that of nature, for it seemed to encompass and transcend all philosophy and spirit, blending to a grand and pure whole. He seemed to possess the wisdom of the ages. His answers to questions, though brief and to the point, were very insightful and powerful. Grandfather was amazed, for he had never before met a man outside of the native cultures that possessed such knowledge. The spirit had led Grandfather to a good place.

Grandfather, Torrence, and Zee spent several days together. Each learned from the other. There grew a sense of brotherhood and friendship that transcended all three cultures. Surely, Grandfather thought, this is how it should be with all people—an equality, a mutual respect, and a deep love for each other. The more time they spent together, the more they realized they all had arrived at the same philosophy of life and spirit, though through different paths. They now walked a common path and spoke a common tongue. This was what the elders had described to Grandfather as the perfect world. The friendship and brotherhood forged there would last a lifetime. The wisdom exchanged was beyond all of Grandfather's hopes and expectations. In the past several days, so much had been answered, so much had been learned, and so many more questions came to light. Grandfather felt that he grew more spiritually in those few days than he had ever grown before in such a short time span.

Torrence departed one morning, telling his brothers that he had to return to his cabin. He could not linger, for the spirit called unto him and he had to obey. Grandfather knew his time was also growing short, and he would soon return to the trail of searching. It was sad to see Torrence go, but Grandfather knew he would see Torrence again. Grandfather remained with Zee for two more days. Each day was spent learning of the other's path that had led him to this place and time of spiritual enlightenment. The paths were so similar that they could be viewed the same, even though they had their origins on opposite sides of the world. Eventually Grandfather stopped sharing and began learning from the ageless wisdom of Zee, for Zee was much older, more traveled, and wiser in the various religions and philosophies of the world. On the last day of his stay Grandfather got the answer he was looking for but could not articulate— the answer to the question of the Sacred Silence.

Early on the last day Zee sat Grandfather down in his garden and came right out and told Grandfather exactly what he needed to know. This shocked Grandfather, because the questions had been unasked and the answers came from nowhere. Zee simply told Grandfather that the Sacred Silence was the same as Zee's meditation, and it was meditation that was the common thread that ran through all religions and philosophies of the world. Though meditation had taken several obscure forms, it was all meditation, some forms more effective than others. Zee said, "Meditation is one of the common threads, the common truths that are part of all. Every religion and philosophy has its form of meditation, but most are obscured by man's dogmas and doctrines, his quest to complicate. Once you understand the elements of meditation, you will then identify the single most important reason why religions are different."

Zee smiled at Grandfather and said, "Meditation, your Sacred Silence, is the pathway to the spiritual mind. It is the vehicle, the bridge that gets us to that place of spirit, purifies the mind, and allows us to live the duality of flesh and spirit. The problem today is that meditation has become for many the end result. Consequently the bridge has become a prison. No matter which philosophy, religion, or approach one takes, there are but four elements to a meditation. The seeker must be comfortable and relaxed, free of the limitations, discomforts, and distractions of the physical body. The seeker must also develop a passive attitude when confronting the distraction that would otherwise remove him from the meditation. Finally, the seeker must have a 'hair,' which is the single most important factor in any meditation, and thus becomes the reason for the major differences in religion."

"A hair?" Grandfather asked.

"Yes, a hair," Zee said. "Let me explain it to you this way, with a story I learned from a man in a faraway place, many years ago. It is important for you to remember that in this story, the uncontrolled demon represents the physical mind. The controlled demon is the spiritual mind."

Zee started to tell Grandfather the ancient story of the Hair and the Demon. Zee began saying, "There was a man who lived alone in the forest. He lived alone because he sought the spiritual ways, but he was missing an important element in becoming a medicine man. Each day he would go out into the forest and seek the knowledge of the spirit, but each day he returned with nothing more than he left with. Then one day, during one of his walks, he spied a sorcerer sitting on a rock in the center of the field, apparently asleep. Now he knew that a sorcerer was a very powerful person, sometimes evil, but his curiosity caused him to draw near. As he crept up behind the sorcerer, he decided to capture him and demand that he give him the secret of being a medicine man, a holy man, and a healer.

"The man fashioned a rope from a vine, stalked closer to the sorcerer, then threw the vine around him and tied him. The sorcerer awoke furious at the man, demanding to be immediately let go. The man would not let him go, not only because he wanted the knowledge of a shaman, but also out of fear for his life. However, the man knew that by universal law he could have the sorcerer grant him one wish and then he would let him go. The man sheepishly told the sorcerer that he would let him go only after his wish was granted. The sorcerer, realizing that there was no other way, told the man that he would have his wish. As the man thought about what he would wish for, the sorcerer grew angrier and angrier, demanding that the man make up his mind. The man sat down and thought long and hard about his wish, which only succeeded in infuriating the sorcerer even more.

"The man, being a very smart man, did not want to wish for money or riches, for he knew that these would only lead to evil. He did not want to wish for food, shelter, happiness, or health, for these things he already possessed. He then asked the sorcerer for a demon, that which is possessed by all shamans, that would do his bidding for the rest of his life and beyond. Now the sorcerer, also being very smart, said 'I will give you a demon, but under one condition. You must keep it busy all of the time, in sleep and while awake; otherwise it will consume you. It will remove you from the ways of the spirit and forever imprison you in the flesh.' It did not take the man long to demand the demon, and the sorcerer nodded his head in agreement. In a flash he was gone, and the man was left standing alone.

"As he walked back home, a small gargoyle-like demon appeared before him and said, 'Master, I am your demon.' The man was taken by surprise, for he thought that the sorcerer had lied about granting him a demon. The man told the demon to follow him home. Once at home, he began to feel tired from his walk and wanted to lie down. Remembering what the sorcerer said about keeping the demon busy, he told the demon to go out and build him a beautiful new house, high up on the hill that overlooked the forest valley where he now lived. The demon smiled and in a flash was gone. The man smiled and lay down to rest. Just as he closed his eyes, there was a flash of light and the demon stood before him. Angry that his rest had been interrupted, he told the demon not to bother him and to get back to the task of building his new home. The demon only smiled at him and said, 'Master, it is done.'

"The man was deeply shocked, for he could not believe the demon could build a house so quickly. He moved to the door and looked out, only to see a beautiful house high on the hill. The demon now demanded that the man give him something to do, and began to grow larger and more fearsome. The man, now frightened at the demon's ability and size, told the demon to furnish the new house, plant beautiful gardens and vineyards, and prepare a feast for all of his friends. The demon again smiled and said, 'Master, it is done. Now give me more to do.' Now the demon grew larger and more fearsome, the man more frightened and desperate. Each time the man gave the demon something to do the demon replied,

'It is done' and grew larger and more menacing. Finally, out of desperation, the man told the demon to heal his sick and dying friend, but again the demon told him, 'It is done.'

"The man was terrified and shaken now. The demon was growing larger and more fearsome with each passing moment. The man could feel his spirit becoming slowly enveloped by the demon. His humanity was being stripped away from him, and his head swooned with the relentless bantering of the demon's voice. There was no escape. No matter how difficult the task, the demon said, 'It is done.' In desperation, the man dived out the window and began running through the woods, until finally he lost the demon. Still running in a blind panic, he ran right into a shaman who had been walking along the path. The man fell to his knees and told the shaman of his plight, of his demon, and of his torment. The shaman smiled down at the man lovingly and said, 'Grandson, we all have our demons.' With that, he plucked a hair from his curly head and handed it to the man, saying, 'Give the demon this hair and tell him to straighten it.'

"The man looked at the curled hair and exclaimed, 'Straighten this hair! My god, you do not know this demon! He can build homes in moments, plan feasts, and heal the sick!' The shaman waved his hand in a gesture of silence and repeated, 'Give him the hair and tell him to straighten it.' Before the man could utter another word, the shaman disappeared in a flash of light. The man was alone again, trembling with fear, shocked with utter disbelief. He could not see what good a curled hair would do in the fight against such a powerful demon. Faced with no other choice, however, he began to walk back to his home. Suddenly the demon appeared before him on the path, larger and more fearsome than he had ever been before. In what sounded like a thousand screaming voices, the demon demanded the man give him something to do. The man stood trembling and frightened, unable to move or even think. His mind was being consumed by the very presence of the demon.

"With his last bit of spiritual strength the man handed the demon the hair and asked him to straighten it. The demon grabbed the hair from the man, smiled at him in an arrogant way, and pulled the hair straight, then smiled at the man triumphantly. Then, as the demon let the hair go, it curled again. The demon subsequently shrunk in size. The demon pulled the hair straight again and let it go, only to have it curl. The demon now grew furious and tried again and again, but to no avail. He could not straighten the hair, and now had shrunk down to his original size. The demon's sheepish manner returned. Upon seeing this, the man grabbed the hair from the demon and told him to carry him home and put him to bed. As soon as the man was in bed, the demon demanded that the man give him something to do. With a broad smile on his face, the man handed the demon the hair and told him to straighten it, and with that fell into a deep and much needed sleep."

At the end of the story, Zee smiled at Grandfather and said, "You see, the hair is but a symbol, a symbol of that final element of meditation. It is the various 'hairs' of man that make religions appear different, but looking deep they are all the same, for they all possess some form of meditation. You know these hairs well, but call them by countless other names. They are the chants, the songs, the rituals, the dogmas, the ceremonies, the drumming, and the countless other religious artifacts that people cling to like crutches. When people see these things, when they become involved in the rituals, their uncontrolled demons are quieted and the spiritual self emerges. If we can learn to get beyond the crutches of the hairs, then the meditations will become simple, pure, and dynamic. The farther man moves toward the flesh and the confines of the physical mind, the more elaborate hairs he needs."

Zee continued without waiting for Grandfather's response, saying, "The problem with meditation today is not only the countless hairs, but the fact that meditation has become an end result, and at best is very sedentary and unusable. People seem to need the complicated crutches of the hair in order to seek spiritual things, thus the meditations are ineffective and confining. In your Sacred Silence you, too, use a hair, but it is not confining or sedentary. Like my form, it is dynamic and usable. You use it now as you listen to me, as you walk the pathless wilderness, but you find it hard to achieve in the company of others. That is why you must continue your search for purity as I continue mine, for I, too, have hairs that must be set aside. Our path to purity must be found and passed on before man smothers and destroys himself under the unbearable weight of his hairs. There is a simpler and purer way."

Grandfather was both shocked and enlightened by Zee's words, for he knew that Zee spoke the truth. Grandfather now knew the answer to his question of the Sacred Silence, and how it could be found in one form or another in all religions and philosophies. He also knew he had to find the simple purity, the simple truth, free of all hairs. Before Grandfather could speak a word, Zee said, "Once all religious hairs are transcended, then all people will walk a common and pure path to spiritual enlightenment. It is possible through each religion and philosophy to reach that place of purity, that which you call the shamanic path. That is why you and I can speak a common tongue, where our hearts beat as one and our minds are of one. We have transcended our religion and beliefs, shed our hairs, and now walk in flesh and spirit."

Zee stood, touched Grandfather on the shoulder, and disappeared into his little house. Grandfather knew it was time for him to go, and he was saddened because he would never again see Zee in the flesh, only in the spirit. Along this shamanic path, Grandfather knew there could be no goodbyes, for here there was no time, no place, and no death. People who walk this path will never be alone, for they are part of each other and are children of the Earth. The sadness disappeared as Grandfather walked away, for he knew that Zee would always be there. Zee had answered many questions that had haunted Grandfather for a long time. Grandfather knew he had helped Zee along his path, also. Any sadness then was for the mindless masses who would forever be imprisoned by their cherished hairs.

5

Philosophy of Choice

As Grandfather began to wander away from Zee's cabin, his mind was deep in thought, so much so that he paid little attention to where he was going. At first he thought of going back to see Torrence, but that was just a fleeting thought with no spiritual foundation or direction. Grandfather certainly missed both Torrence and Zee even though he was not yet gone a day. So, too, did he miss his people, but there was work he had to do. The driving spirit would not allow him to rest. He had to find answers to the purity and to many other things that remained yet unasked. He wandered again for several days, but nothing more was revealed to him. However, he had thought through and internalized all that he had learned, and now even more than before, he understood what made all people the same but different. Now there was no room for any prejudice, for the end result of all paths was that which the elders called the shamanic path.

Ironically Grandfather's path wound in a huge circle, coming back to where the journey began, at the cabin of Torrence. He walked up to greet Torrence, who sat on the floor next to his rocking chair. Torrence seemed to know why he was there, but Grandfather had no idea why he had come back. However, Torrence did not want to say anything at first. Instead, they discussed fully what Zee had told Grandfather. It was that same story of the hair that led Torrence away from the White man's ways and to the path he now walked. Torrence, in all his subsequent years of searching, admitted to Grandfather that he had not found the simpler and purer way. He, like Grandfather and Zee, still searched for that simple purity that seemed to be forever out of reach. So, too, did he still use wilderness and aloneness as a hair.

Torrence told Grandfather it was easy to walk the shamanic path when alone in the purity of wilderness. It became difficult to walk that path in the company of common man. There was always the demonic destruction of their flesh, which seemed to infect anyone who was walking in spirit. That is one of the reasons he now chose to live alone. Torrence thought he must find that simple purity first in aloneness and then integrate it into his daily life. Only then could he ever hope to bring it back to the masses. Even living with Zee would produce a distraction, and though mild, it would still retard the search and cloud the mind. Grandfather, thinking out loud, said, "Then if this simple truth cannot yet be found, possibly we search in the wrong place. For all too long I have been looking outside of myself. Does it not then stand to reason that the way can be found only within one's heart and spirit? That seems to be where my search takes me now, to the vast uncharted regions of my spiritual mind."

The words seemed to come from nowhere. It startled Grandfather to hear that wisdom spoken by his own voice. Only when he finally articulated it to another did he realize that his wanderings, all these years, were actually journeys into self, disguised as physical journeys. Even Torrence was awestruck by Grandfather's sudden wisdom. Torrence saw that Grandfather's face had the look of startled satisfaction, and Grandfather saw the same look on Torrence's face. They both laughed long and hard. It was obvious that Grandfather's words had been directed by a force far outside himself, or from deep within. Regardless of where the wisdom came from, it was something they both desperately needed to know and hear. The search had to be directed inwardly, not outwardly. "We cannot carry with us always the hair of aloneness and wilderness, or for that matter, any other hair," Grandfather said, again thinking out loud. "We must carry with us something simple and pure that will always be with us, despite the distractions. Something that can only be found inside, and thus is always there."

The ensuing silence seemed to last forever as Grandfather and Torrence contemplated these words. They both knew they were onto something special, on the verge of a grand enlightenment, but they could not yet put it into any words or usable concepts. It was like knowing without knowing how you know. The more they thought about this concept of internal hairs, the more distant the solution seemed to become. They both agreed that the solution was probably so simple and pure that they were overlooking it while trying to complicate the answer. As Grandfather thought about the probable simplicity of it all, he began to feel that the answer must be found somewhere in the logical, physical mind itself. He wondered if instead of looking at the physical mind only as an enemy, could it be that the physical mind, or at least part of it, was also an ally?

Grandfather conveyed his feelings to Torrence, and Torrence wholeheartedly agreed. Grandfather said, "We were all born to live the duality. However, in most people, the logical mind becomes dominant, for it is trained the most. In my people, it is important to train both minds. A child becomes equally versed in the wisdom of the physical mind and the wisdom of the spiritual mind. It is only when the physical mind becomes overtrained, as it is with most people, that it becomes dominant. Yet there is still part of the physical mind that remains connected to the spiritual mind. It is that part of the physical mind that guides many to seek the wisdom of the spirit. Thus the solution must lie within the friendly part of the logical mind. This part must contain the internal 'hair' that triggers the logical mind to quiet, and thus allows the spiritual mind to come forth. What then could be the internal hair?"

Grandfather and Torrence discussed this possibility well into the night, barely taking time for any breaks or even to eat. They were so engrossed and enthusiastic over the possibilities that they became too excited to do anything else. They both told stories about people they knew who were once so wrapped up in the logical, physical mind that they never would be inclined to seek the wisdom of the spirit. Yet, despite the odds being against them, one day they would turn around and begin the journey along their spiritual path. So then, there must be something in that part of the physical mind that would ultimately direct us to seek spiritual ways. It is that same part of a person's mind that wonders if there is more to life than just the flesh. Both exhausted from the searching process, Grandfather and Torrence decided to get some sleep and begin again in the morning. The sleep would be a way of clarifying what they had discussed and learned.

Grandfather fell into a state somewhere between sleep and awake. His dream mind wandered over all the journeys of the quest for purity he had undertaken in the past several moons. Coyote Thunder had been right. It was in the span of just one moon that the greatest enlightenment had come to Grandfather. What followed now was a reinforcement of what he learned, and the chance to discover the truth of the last remaining details. It seemed that all of the spiritual quests in his life had led him right to this point in time and place. Now all he needed were the final answers so he could put it all to use. It was not long before Grandfather fell into a deep and much needed sleep. However, several times during the night he awakened without cause, sat up and looked around, then just as suddenly fell back to sleep. Each time he awoke, he felt as if he was reaching out for something, but once he was fully awake, it was no longer there.

It was during the last abrupt awakening that Grandfather saw the old woman again. She smiled at him warmly and said, "So you have come this far, yet you still have one last quest to work through. Once you arrive at that truth, your spiritual path in life will change, and you will then seek to gather all manner of spiritual knowledge, now in a pure way. You wonder what the bridge must be between the logical conscious and the spiritual mind. As you have decided, there is a simple and pure answer. That answer will come to you once you have discovered the secret."

"But what is that secret?" Grandfather asked.

"It is simple, so simple, for you have known it all along," said the old woman. "Once I reveal the secret unto you, I will leave you until the day you pass to the spirit world. My work with you will be done. What you seek is simply choice." And with that she was gone.

Grandfather sat up abruptly only to find that Torrence was also sitting up. They both looked at each other and said simultaneously, "Choice," and laughed almost out of control. Grandfather told Torrence of the old woman and how she had directed him on the search for purity from the very beginning, and now had told Grandfather that the answer lay in the concept of choice. Torrence told Grandfather that he, too, had a dream of an old man who told him to use choice as the doorway to seek the answers they were looking for. Both agreed that choice was a good place to start, for a person had to make the choice to walk the spiritual path before everything else would fall into place. It was decided that each of them would share what they knew of choice, but other than making the choice to walk a spiritual path, Torrence was at a loss for what to say.

Grandfather, on the other hand, had already begun to decipher the idea of choice. He said, "Coyote Thunder used to tell me when I was very young that there were many actions on a physical level that had implications in the spirit world. I learned when I was very young that I had the luxury of choice in whatever I did. I learned that only I could choose whether I was to be happy or sad. It was only through my choice that I could create a heaven or hell out of any situation. I could blame no one else for my own happiness or despair, my path, my life, or my situation. It was all up to me to make the right choices. Outside circumstances did not matter to me, for I could not easily change them. What I learned to do was to choose happiness, and no one could do that for me. Through choice, Coyote Thunder taught me that I was in control of my own destiny. Survival living also teaches us that we have choice. If we are cold, then we build fire or shelter. If we are thirsty, then we find water, and if we are hungry, we forage or hunt. What is true in survival is also true in all of life—our mind, our choices, make us happy or sad. If we waited for outside circumstances to be perfect, then we would rarely be happy. We must choose happiness no matter what the circumstances. Only we have that power, and no one else can decide for us."

Grandfather paused for a long moment in a deep and thoughtful manner, then continued, saying, "Many people believe that our lives are planned, but I do not believe this to be so. The Great Spirit has given all things a choice, and thus the future does not yet exist, nor is it planned. If the future were planned, then we would have no choice. Thus the future is like the hand. The palm of the hand is our now, and the fingers are the possible futures. It is through our choices that we decide which road or future is taken. It is through our choices that we abandon one road and go to the next. However, there is always one stronger and more defined pathway leading away from the palm of the now, and this we call the probable future. Yet no matter how probable that future may seem, we are still in control through our choices.

"I know the Creator has given us choice and not a planned future," Grandfather continued. "But what are our choices in life and in spirit? Well, first we must understand what major choices we have, and this is a simple undertaking. We can choose good, we can choose evil, or we can choose neither. There are but three choices. Once the Creator gave us the option of choice, there became no set future, just these three choices. We are also given a choice to walk a good spiritual path, an evil spiritual path, or to dwell fully in the flesh. Some people will deny that evil exists for fear of giving it power, but denying that evil exists does not make it go away, for it has power on its own. With this choice also comes the physical battles of good and evil, which in turn cause the battles of good and evil spirits. Once one accepts the fact that we all have choice, then one must also accept these three choices. All other choices come from these three."

Torrence sat captivated by Grandfather's conversation. He had never thought of choice in that way. He had always assumed that he had been guided to the path he now walked, but as he came to understand choice, he realized he had actually chosen that path. However, neither he or Grandfather knew what choice had to do with the doorway to the spirit, other than exercising a choice to follow its power. Torrence and Grandfather talked for a long time about the idea of choice but still could not arrive at any viable conclusion. Possibly it was because again they were trying too hard and making it far too complicated. Could it be, Grandfather thought, that it is the choice itself which is the "hair" we are seeking? Could it be that we could willingly choose to set aside our logical minds and allow our spiritual minds to come forth? Is it this choice that will replace all hairs?

Grandfather began to think about the way he entered the sacred silence through the "hair" of nature and creation. He then realized there first must be a choice to enter the sacred silence, even before using nature as a hair. If he could find a way to make this choice his "hair," then truly it would become an internal process. Then he could live in spirit any time, any place, or in any situation. He told Torrence what he was thinking, but Torrence did not respond. He just stared blankly at the earth between them. Finally Torrence said, "In my heart I know you are right, but I do not think the answers will be found through our words. We are born alone and we will die alone. Thus we can only seek those personal answers alone, for each spiritual path is unique. The more we talk, the more complicated we make the philosophy of choice." Grandfather wholeheartedly agreed and was gone by the next morning.

Grandfather began his long journey back to his people, feeling now that this was where his spirit directed him. His mind would not let go of all that he had learned, especially the question of choice and all that surrounded it. All through the first day and well into the night, he was locked deep in thought, and even his dreams would not let go of the searching process. By the second day of his journey, even with a full night's sleep, he was mentally exhausted. He also became angry at himself in a way, for he knew that the solution must be so simple that he was overlooking it. So, too, was he angry due to all of his mental searching, he had missed so much of the natural beauty that could be found along his walk. But no matter how much he tried, he could not get the searching process out of his mind.

In desperation, and needing a mental break very badly, Grandfather decided to stop his journey and sit down for a while with the purpose of freeing himself of his questions. He knew from past experience that the best way to do this was to slip into a deep Sacred Silence, making his spiritual mind dominant and putting aside his physical mind. After all, it was the physical mind that was involved in all of the searching.

He found a beautiful place right by a small stream and sat down there to rest. He let go of his thoughts for a while, quieting his internal waters so to speak, and began to slip into a deep Sacred Silence, deeper than he normally walked within. As he felt the power of the Sacred Silence overwhelm him, he was suddenly awestruck. It was through the process of reaching the Sacred Silence in a purposeful way that the question of choice was answered.

Grandfather had no idea why or how he had overlooked something that he had used all his life—the wisdom of choice and what lies beyond. The simplicity of it all hit Grandfather like a cold splash of water. Without delay he hurried back to Torrence. He wanted to share his insight with Torrence so Torrence would not be restricted to the basic search. Grandfather also wanted to discuss this insight together and possibly go beyond that which Grandfather now understood.

He could not believe that he and Torrence had overlooked something so obvious, when all along they both used this internal "hair," but could not isolate and identify it. It had been there all along, staring them right in the spiritual face, yet they overlooked it because they tried to complicate the answer. Grandfather headed directly to Torrence's cabin, taking no time to sleep, eat, or drink.

When Grandfather arrived at the cabin the next morning, Torrence was sitting in his rocking chair as usual. He did not seem surprised that Grandfather had returned. That was obvious when he told Grandfather that he had expected him. Torrence said, "I knew that it would not take you long to find us the answers we needed, though I didn't expect you back so soon!" Grandfather did not hesitate but immediately began to tell Torrence what he had found. Grandfather said, "We have both used the power of choice to begin the process of entering the spirit world. But we both assumed that we used the wilderness as a vehicle that would produce the Sacred Silence, thus we assumed that creation was our hair. Not so. Yes, possibly at first, when I was a child, I used creation, but now I use the internal hair, and up until this time did not know it."

Grandfather continued, "We were both perplexed over the idea that there must be a part of our physical mind that was directly connected to the spiritual, but we did not know how to use it or how it worked. We just knew that it must be there. We also assumed it was this part of our physical mind that would bring us to spiritual consciousness after we made the 'choice' to do so. Well, we use that part of our mind all the time. It was so simple that we both overlooked its power, its simplicity, and exactly how we used it. It is like learning something when you are very young and forgetting how you learned. You use that something so often that it becomes natural and you assume it has always been there. And so it was with the simple wisdom and the internal 'hair' that lies beyond choice."

Grandfather could tell that Torrence was getting impatient with all of this explanation, so he got right to the point. He said, "As I began my walk back to my people, I began to think about the way that I use my Inner Vision, how it guides me, how it protects me, and how it links me directly to my spiritual self. I know that this Inner Vision is the direct communication between my physical self and the world of the spirit-that-moves-in-all-things, the spirit world, and is in fact the very voice of the Creator. I thought then of the way this communication is passed unto me. It is not in words, for the worlds beyond the physical self do not understand the tongues of man, only the tongues of heart. So the Inner Vision communicates to us in signs, symbols, dreams, visions, and feelings, mostly feelings. There are no words, for it knows no words."

Grandfather paused as he gathered his thoughts, then continued. "So if the worlds outside of our physical selves communicate to us in these signs, symbols, visions, dreams, and feelings, then we must do the same to communicate with those same worlds. We cannot do so in words, so we must use the same language as Inner Vision, and send it to those outer worlds."

Torrence excitedly said, "Yes. I use that form of conveyance all the time, not only to bring forth my form of Sacred Silence but also to send messages to the spirit world and beyond."

Grandfather continued, smiling with satisfaction that Torrence agreed, and said, "When I send a message to the spirit world, I first must see what I want in my mind, give it power, and then send it beyond with a firm belief that it is so, it is done. I also hold the picture in my mind when I enter the Sacred Silence, so it is the image that we hold in our mind that gives us the 'hair' and the power."

Grandfather, now just letting the words flow, said, "It is the part of our physical mind that creates the image that releases the spirit and sends the message to the world of nature and spirit. All of this time we carried that internal 'hair' with us, but it was so simple, so commonplace, that we took it for granted, thus overlooking its power. So then, the Sacred Silence is not reachable unless first we make a choice and then create the image. And the image remains powerless unless we empower it with an unwavering faith. So, too, do I feel there is more, but at least we now know the basic and simple answer we have been searching for." Torrence nodded his head in thoughtful agreement, though he appeared to burn with another question. Grandfather felt a little uneasy, for he now wondered if Torrence was only agreeing to be nice.

Finally Torrence looked at Grandfather and said, "I agree with everything you say, but I now feel that it must be proven. This all may work for you and for me, but can it work for all others? As you told me, we must take things to creation and test them out there. If they work there and work for everyone, then they are truth. We have not yet tested this in the worlds of man, and what we now have to do is put it to the ultimate test and teach someone who is not spiritually inclined. Let us go forth and find a willing student, and then meet back here in two moons." Grandfather smiled in agreement, for he knew that Torrence spoke the truth. Unless something could be fully tested, then it was only theory and not law. Grandfather's path was now clear, for he knew what he had to do. Before dawn of the next day he was gone.

6

Moses

Grandfather once again headed back to his people. His mind was now clear of all the thoughts that had filled it, and he was free to enjoy the magic of creation that surrounded him. He was concerned, however, about the difficulty of finding the proper student to test his new theory. He could not use one of his own people, for many of them were already traveling a highly spiritual path. This created a problem, for he knew of no one outside of his tribe that was not spiritually oriented. The thought of finding someone from the outside world nearly terrified him, yet it was something that he had to do. Unless his philosophy worked for an outsider, then it was not a truth, and only worked for him. His philosophy then would be no better than other, more complicated philosophies.

As Grandfather wandered, his mind became even more engrossed in the search to find a student. He knew that if his theory worked for this student, it would work for anyone. It would thus allow anyone to immediately enter the spirit world, to communicate with the spirit-that-moves-in-all-things, to create miracles, and to begin the journey of enlightenment. Essentially, it would allow a person to transcend any religion, even his own. In fact, if a person so wanted, he or she would not have to give up the basic doctrine or teachings of their religion, but use Grandfather's simple philosophy to enhance its power. That in essence would be the final test—to see if a holy man or woman from another philosophy or religion could integrate Grandfather's philosophy into his or her own. Then Grandfather's philosophy truly would be a universal truth.

Grandfather began to consider the far-reaching ramifications that his philosophy could have on a person's individual spiritual path. He thought about all the time he had spent studying the various religions and learning their customs, traditions, ceremonies, doctrines, and basic laws. If in fact a person could learn Grandfather's philosophy and put it to use, then years—no decades—could be taken off their spiritual career. He knew that in his own belief system a child began spiritual training when he or she was very young, some no more than six years old, and by being taught by a medicine man or woman. The child stayed with that shaman until he was in his twentieth winter, learning the skills, and philosophies, administering healing herbs, and taking part in the ceremonies as an apprentice. He then would be required to live an ascetic life for many years, learning firsthand from nature's spirit. Next, he would return to the shaman for several more years of learning, until finally he could work on his own. Many did not reach this point until they were well thirty to forty winters old. Only then could they begin to transcend their own path and walk the common path of the shaman. Using Grandfather's way, however, a person could walk that path in less than a moon.

Thinking about the possibility literally overwhelmed Grandfather. Now he was even more determined to find a willing student. So, too, did he begin to wonder why no one had arrived at this philosophy before. It was not that difficult, yet he had been practicing this simplicity since he was a child. As far back as he could remember, he rarely used the ceremonies that his people used. Instead, he would reach the same spiritual level as did his elders but in this simpler and purer way. They, on the other hand, spent hours and sometimes days getting to the same spiritual place Grandfather could reach in moments. Even Coyote Thunder still used ceremony, though not as heavily as did the rest. That did not mean Grandfather felt these ceremonies had no power, for they certainly did, and he gave them as much respect as anyone. Somehow he had stumbled onto a simpler way.

Grandfather did not feel worthy enough to have arrived at this simple philosophy; in fact he felt a little guilty. He thought that it should have been Coyote Thunder or one of the other elders, not he. After all, Grandfather was barely into his twenty-sixth winter. Certainly he always had a deeper spiritual drive than most of his peers and continuously sought the wisdom of the spirit from as far back as he could remember, but this did not make him feel worthy of such a powerful discovery. He began to wonder if for some reason the spirit world had helped him on his lifelong spiritual search. But why did the spirit world single him out, and not a more worthy individual, such as Coyote Thunder, who had dedicated nearly ninety winters to spiritual quests? For some reason he had been chosen, and he did not know why.

Again the question of where to find a student hammered into his thoughts. He had no idea where to begin to look. He prayed that a student would be sent to him, and turned the whole searching process over to the spirit and the Creator. If in fact he had been helped and guided to this simple truth by the spirit world, then they would also send him a student. If no one was found, he had to assume that this simple philosophy was his alone, until proven otherwise. Just because it worked well for him did not mean it would work for anyone else. Possibly his philosophy could not be learned, and just maybe he was someone special to the spirit world, as Coyote Thunder had so often told him. But what good would this philosophy be if Grandfather could not pass it down to others? Spiritual selfishness was foreign to his way of thinking. He wanted the duality of flesh and spirit to be possible for anyone and everyone.

Exhaustion finally caught up with Grandfather, and he decided to make camp and stay for several days to regain his strength and clear his mind. The area he chose for a camp was so beautiful that it defied description. This rich and fertile mountain forest was a monument to the Creator's love. A small but pretty waterfall danced down the face of the rocks and sang the song of life. Everywhere was the intensity of living energy, where all things sang their praises to the Great Spirit. It was a perfect place to purge the mind, relax the body, and to pray. Here Grandfather felt close to the Creator and to creation. This place would provide a much welcome and needed reprieve from the learning and searching process, for it was truly an oasis of tranquility and love. No sooner had he made camp than he fell into a deep sleep.

Coyote Thunder came to Grandfather in his dreams, in a very unexpected way. Grandfather dreamed of many people dancing and chanting around a huge fire. Drummers played, elders prayed, and everyone seemed spiritually caught up in the intensity of the ceremony. Grandfather, too, began to get caught up in the power of the ceremony and drawn closer to the spirit. From out of the crowds walked Coyote Thunder, directly to where Grandfather sat. Coyote Thunder wore his coyote headdress, his painted buckskins, and carried his rattle and pipe. He stood before Grandfather and said, "As I have told you, these ceremonies are not for you. Your path, your Vision, is to simplify the spiritual complications of man. You then must find a way to teach this simple truth to all who will listen. For now and for the rest of your physical life, your Vision is to simplify, simplify." Grandfather then awoke to the first light of dawn.

Coyote Thunder did not tell Grandfather something he did not know, but just reinforced and clarified his path. Yet the dream caused Grandfather to take a long and hard look at what he assumed to be his Vision. Up until now, he thought that his overall Vision encompassed many things. But as he scrutinized his Vision, he realized that no matter how he looked at it, his Vision was to simplify. Yes, he wanted to learn all of the old ways he could and preserve them. He also wanted to learn and practice all he could of tracking and awareness. In addition, he wanted to learn as much as he could about other philosophies, beliefs, and religions, but more important, he had to simplify these concepts and teach that simplicity. All roads, all visions, seemed to lead to that simplicity, and in that simplicity lay an awesome power.

Grandfather spent the next several days exploring the area around his camp. He took short and long journeys out onto the land. Some only lasted a few hours, but some lasted all day and well into the night. He began to let go of all the questions. His strength returned, the peace returned, and he became caught up in the splendor of nature. The search for spiritual purity and awareness was not an easy one. All too often he would neglect to sleep or eat, forcing himself on to the distant answers. Fatigue only produced an obscurity, so it was important for Grandfather to know when he had reached his limits mentally and emotionally. That is why this time of wandering was so important to him. It is in this time of recovery, where the mind is set free from the searching path, that real answers come, unrestricted and absolute. Wilderness became the catalyst of purification.

Grandfather could feel a sense of wonder as he walked the line between flesh and spirit. For every physical action there was a spiritual reaction. Nature, too, became a duality, where the superficial flesh of the forest was transcended and the reality of its spiritual existence became manifest. All too often in his searching, Grandfather would look beyond nature and dwell sometimes too much in the things of the spirit. He realized that he must be more aware of the things around him rather than be so absorbed in himself. By focusing solely on the problem at hand, locked into thought, one was removed from the pure and natural world. The solutions to problems then become obscured by self, and almost totally out of reach. That is why Grandfather would so often let go of a problem and immerse himself into the natural world. For it was there in nature that the solutions to internal searching would come purely and easily.

As Grandfather wandered up along the edge of a tiny stream, he heard a faint crying. At first he thought that it originated from the world of spirit, but upon further searching found that it came from within a small valley, off to the side of where he was wandering. Following the stream slowly and carefully, he began to draw closer to the origin of the sound. The crying sounded so mournful and so painful, so out of place in this temple of creation. The little valley began to widen slightly and give way to smaller trees and shrubs, affording Grandfather a clear view of what lay ahead. In the distance the valley opened wide, revealing the rock-strewn slope of a cliff. High up in the rocks Grandfather could see evidence of a recent gold mine apparently still active. It was from the mouth of this mine that the crying originated.

Grandfather wanted to end his search right here. There was no way he wanted to venture any closer, for the mine foretold of the White man's presence and the gold of evil. He knew from past experience that the White man defended these mines and would kill any trespassers that ventured near. However, the crying was so intense that Grandfather became torn between helping or retreating. Inner Vision began to tell Grandfather to help, but his fear was such that the last few hundred yards of his travel was a slow cautious stalk. The crying continued on and off throughout the entire journey, which now seemed to take forever. So, too, was it necessary for Grandfather to push his senses hard, and this hypervigilance was exhausting and stressful. Finally he got close enough to the mine to clearly see all that was around its mouth.

Near the mine was a small shack where various strange tools were strewn about in random disorder. A small fenced compound held two old mules, and around the shack were several chickens and an old dog. There was no evidence of any large number of White men, just the tracks of one man. The tracks confirmed that there was only one person living in the shack and working the mine. These tracks foretold of the man's advanced years, a bent back from hard work, and the onset of painful arthritis. Grandfather also noted that there were things around the shack that would normally belong to a woman, but they were in such dusty shape that he knew a woman had not been there in quite a long time. He wondered if she had died there, but upon scrutinizing the outskirts of the compound, he could find no evidence of a grave.

With the utmost caution Grandfather stalked closer to the shack. It was obvious that the crying was coming from the far side, probably from an old wood shed that was attached to the house. He drew close to the house, peering through the window and past the old curtains that still hung from the frame. The house was neat but dusty, sparsely furnished, and rather tattered and worn with use. There, too, was more evidence of a woman's presence, but again there was indication that she was no longer around and hadn't been for quite some time. The interior of the cabin also confirmed Grandfather's first beliefs that there was but one old man living here. Just as Grandfather was moving away and to the rear of the woodshed, he spied a picture near an old woodstove. The picture was of a Black family, apparently taken in the forests of the East, but like everything else the picture appeared very old.

By the time Grandfather approached the rear of the shed, the crying had softened to a mournful moan, sometimes barely a sobbing. He edged his way to a rather large crack in the rear of the structure and peered inside. There on the ground sat an older Black man, tears dried on his face, bearing the expression of pain. It was evident from the tracks around him that the old man had sat there for better than a full day. Grandfather could not understand why the old man had been there for so long, seated in that very place. As Grandfather shifted his position for a better look, he could see an old revolver lying beside the man, and his heart leapt into his throat. He slumped to the ground silently and planned his retreat. But just as Grandfather began to move from the back of the shed, he heard the man's hoarse cry, a definite and pathetic plea for help that bordered on exhaustion.

Grandfather stopped and turned back to the crack in the shed. With the difference in angle, he could now see that the man's hand was firmly held in some sort of machine. Dried blood was all around the man's hand and on the table, indicating the man had been caught for a long time. Grandfather watched in horror as the old man began to sob again and slowly lifted the gun to his head and pulled back the hammer. Without thinking, Grandfather sprang to his feet and rushed around the shed yelling at the old man to stop. As he turned the corner, Grandfather found himself looking down the barrel of the gun, which stopped him in his tracks. He trembled in sheer terror as he looked into the old man's eyes. The old man, too, was visibly shaken and full of trembling fear. Neither moved for what seemed to be an eternity. Grandfather felt that he was standing on the edge of death.

The old man finally spoke, but Grandfather could barely understand what he said. All Grandfather knew was that he was in danger and that the old man feared him as much as Grandfather feared the old Black man's gun. Grandfather knew that this man probably thought that Grandfather was going to kill him. Grandfather's compassion for the old man far exceeded his fear, and he gently motioned to the old man's hand stuck in the machine. The old man must have sensed Grandfather's compassion, for as soon as Grandfather had spoken, the old man dropped the gun and started to sob. Grandfather knew that this old one was not used to holding a gun or threatening anyone. Grandfather, still cautious, moved toward the old man and looked at his jammed hand. He had no idea how to free him or what the machine was used for. The old man feebly pointed to a lever at the far end of the machine and then made an arcing motion toward the roof.

Grandfather approached the lever, grasped it in his hand and looked back toward the old Black man. The old man pointed at the roof again. Grandfather began to try to push the lever, but it would not budge. Again and again he tried, but there was no movement. He looked back toward the old Black man, now with a worried expression on his face. In a flurry of sign language and broken speech, they began to communicate. Apparently, Grandfather had to lift up the lever so the machine would release the man's hand. Grandfather drew all of his strength into his gut and let go of his mind, thus releasing the primal animal within him. Instantly the lever was lifted high and the machine opened, releasing the man's bloody hand. Blood began to pour from his wound, and the pain was so excruciating that the man cried out.

Grandfather helped the old man to his feet and to the shack. The man could barely stand, and for the final few steps Grandfather just about had to carry him. Grandfather sat the old one down on the edge of the bed and tore a curtain from the window and wrapped it around the man's hand. He then rushed to the hand pump and drew a bucket of water for the old man. Grandfather knew the man would be dehydrated from the amount of time he had spent trapped in the machine and from the loss of blood. Grandfather soaked another curtain in the water and rewrapped the old man's hand, making sure that he was laying down and comfortable. He then told the old man that he was going out to get some medicinal herbs, and the old one seemed to understand. There was no longer fear in the man's eyes, and he felt a certain sense of peace and gratitude toward Grandfather. However, the man still had a slight sense of disbelief that an Indian would be so kind, especially to an old Black man.

For the next several days Grandfather nursed the old man back to health. His hand was not broken, just badly damaged by the gears of the machine. His cuts healed quickly, and he began to regain his strength. Grandfather provided him with plenty of food, and during the times the old man slept, which were frequent, Grandfather cleaned up around the cabin and the yards. Within five suns the old man was fully back on his feet. The communications between him and Grandfather were becoming more fluid and understandable. As the old one grew stronger, Grandfather and he began to take short walks around the compound, going farther and farther afield every day. Once the old man tried to show Grandfather his mine, but Grandfather refused, telling him that he would not enter an unnatural wound in the flesh of Earth Mother. The old man seemed to understand and did not pursue the issue any further.

As time passed, Grandfather and the old man began to communicate with more certainty and clarity. Grandfather found out that the old man was called Moses. Moses grew up on a slave farm in the Deep South, and when he was finally given his freedom after the war, he moved here to the West to seek his fortune. As far back as Moses could remember, he was poor by the White man's standards. He had difficulty finding enough food to eat, and he could not remember a time in his life that he did not have to struggle. Being Black also condemned him to a life of prejudice, ridicule, and low-paying jobs. He was considered by many Whites as no better than a mule. He moved West many years ago thinking that he would escape the prejudice and possibly get some land to farm. Unfortunately, the only land he could get failed after just a few short years.

During this life of poverty, Moses saw both of his sons die. One of them was killed by a local farmer over a water dispute. The other son died of a disease. His wife had stayed with him for only a few years after their sons' deaths. She could not take the rugged life in the mountains, nor his dreams of finding gold. One day she eventually left him without a word while he was working deep in his mine. Now for nearly a decade he had been alone. And he was alone, except for a few other miners who infrequently came to visit. These were not real friends, however, for all they wanted was to see if his mine was productive. If he ever found any gold, they would probably kill him and lay claim to his mine. He even told Grandfather that he thought God had abandoned him and had sentenced him to a life of struggle and misery. He also said that he had been considering suicide for a very long time, such was his pain and need to escape.

As Grandfather listened to Moses' story, he felt a certain kinship to him, for Grandfather had felt the same persecution from the Whites. In fact, Moses told Grandfather that he had been his first real friend, for Grandfather had wanted nothing from him. For the first time in as long as Moses could remember, he could finally talk to someone, and call him friend. Grandfather seemed to understand Moses' pain and really listened to him as one human to another. Within a short few days, Moses and Grandfather became close friends. Grandfather could see a marked and dramatic change in Moses, not only in personality, but in vitality. Moses shifted from a bitter and defeated old man to a man of hope. A certain bounce began to appear in his step, and he seemed to have an enthusiasm for living that Grandfather had not seen in the first few days they were together.

What really troubled Grandfather was that Moses had lost faith in his God. Grandfather also feared that Moses would return to working his mine after Grandfather left, and eventually fall back into the same old trap he had lived in for so long. Grandfather wanted to teach him another way, his way, and possibly show the old man that the true riches in life were found within one's self and not in some worthless pit, digging for the gold that rots men's souls. Grandfather saw Moses as one who had been lured by the fanatical dreams of the White man to a world where he did not really belong. He could tell that Moses was a dreamer, but not a dreamer of the false gods of the flesh. Moses was a dreamer of a world beyond the flesh, for Grandfather could see in him a faint yearning for spiritual wisdom. All Grandfather had to do was get him out of the White man's traps and away from the White man's dreams of the riches of flesh. He had to show Moses how to find hope, real hope, for probably the first time in Moses' life.

So as Moses' hand began to heal completely and his strength fully returned, he and Grandfather began to wander deep into the surrounding mountains. Moses seemed to become a child again, showing more and more enthusiasm with each journey into the wilderness. Moses became an eager student of the wilderness and seemed to be a very willing student. He once admitted to Grandfather that in all the years he had spent in these mountains, he never really knew them or took the time to explore. He had always been so imprisoned in the darkness of the mine, so driven by the flesh, that he had no time for anything else. In those times he did get out into the wilderness, it was only for meat or materials he needed to perpetuate the dream of finding gold. As Moses saw it, the mine and the lust for riches had cost him the lives of his two sons and the woman he loved so dearly.

There began a metamorphosis in their friendship. Where they began as friends, Moses soon looked to Grandfather as a teacher and sage, though Grandfather was many years his junior. It was not long before Moses began to ask Grandfather to teach him how to survive as easily as he did. As the days moved into months, Moses grew more and more adept at survival, until he became a true child of the wilderness. Grandfather began to use the temples of nature and survival as a vehicle to lead Moses back to the wisdom of the spirit, and eventually back to the Creator. Moses began to lose interest altogether in the things of the flesh and cared little to go back into his shack. Moses seemed the most happy and at peace when he was out with Grandfather deep in the wilderness and living in a primitive camp.

Grandfather began to carefully and lovingly lead Moses back to the purity of the spirit. He led Moses to the deep understanding that life was more than just that of physical riches and the toils of the flesh. Grandfather taught Moses there was a greater dimension beyond the false gods of the flesh, attainable by all mankind. Moses began to realize that he had been trapped by the dream of flesh-oriented riches that had caused him to sacrifice his very soul. Little by little, Grandfather began to lead Moses away from the false gods of the flesh and into the power and riches of the spirit. The wilderness became Moses' temple, and the riches of the spirit became his quest. He began to transcend his old self and become a man true to his own heart.

Grandfather taught Moses how to follow the dreams of his heart, to trust his Inner Vision, and to penetrate the world of spirit in a dynamic way. Grandfather could now clearly see the shift in Moses from the flesh to the spirit, then finally to the Creator. A sparkle appeared in Moses' eye and a purpose was found in his step. He seemed a man on the verge of enlightenment, rekindling an old and almost forgotten dream. Then one day, as Grandfather walked to his sacred prayer area high up in the mountains, he passed by the mine. To his amazement, the mine's entrance was boarded up and all the mining tools were in a neat pile. He knew then that Moses had abandoned all senseless dreams of the flesh and now was truly on a spiritual path. Grandfather knew that Moses would never return to that prison of the soul.

When Grandfather returned to the shack after his daily prayers, he found that Moses had packed up his things and appeared ready to leave. Before Grandfather could say a word, Moses said, "I once had a dream that was almost forgotten. I once wanted to become a minister, for I once was close to God. Now that I can see God again in all of His creation, I want to live that old dream. So now I must leave this place and find the woman who loved me so long ago, for it was her dream, too. I have been such a fool all of these years. I have sacrificed everything for the dream of riches, only to find that riches are but temporary and illusive. Only the riches of the spirit are real, and all else is but an illusion. I cannot hesitate on my journey, dear friend, for I have wasted so many years. I will waste no more. I will always be thankful to you for leading me back to my dreams and to the power of the spirit." With that, Moses hugged Grandfather and left on the journey of the rest of his life.

Grandfather watched Moses disappear into the distance. The feeling of loss was far exceeded by the rapture of triumph. Grandfather had found that the wisdom and purity of the spirit could be had by all. In a few short months, he had taken a man from the pits of despair and suicide to the rapture of the spirit. Grandfather saw that what he had taught did not lead the man from his basic beliefs, but enhanced and enlightened them. Grandfather now knew that his philosophy of purity would work for anyone, for it was a philosophy and purity known to all and it produced the much needed "reproducible results." Now Grandfather

knew what he would have to do in the many years to come:
He would have to further purify what he had learned, and
seek the many common threads that bind all philosophies
and religions together. He would have to seek the simple
purity, the profound truth.

PART TWO

THE
WISDOM

Before I met him, Grandfather had wandered for nearly sixty-three years of his life searching for the simple and pure truth. Almost immediately he began to teach me the ways of the spirit. In fact, Rick, Grandfather's blood grandson, and I got our first lesson in the first hour of the first day that I met him. Even though the wisdom of the spirit was more important to him than anything else, he never forced this upon us, but rather allowed us to arrive at the spiritual teachings naturally. As always, and right from the onset, he used the wisdom of nature, survival skills, tracking, and awareness as vehicles that would bring us to the power of the spirit. Each physical skill that he taught, especially that of awareness, had a farther reaching spiritual overtone and deep philosophical meaning. In fact, I cannot remember any skill that did not embody some important teaching of the spirit.

More important, Grandfather would not complicate the spiritual skills. After all, his Vision was not only to find the basic and pure truth, but to simplify that truth. Any complication that we did encounter was of our own doing.

We, like so many other seekers, could not believe that these spiritual truths could be so simple and free. Like many, we believed that we had to suffer to make it worthwhile, for without suffering, we assumed, how could it be powerful? It did not take us long to realize that this is what so many of the great religions and philosophies of the world were in fact doing. The leaders of these religions and philosophies believed, and led the followers to believe, that one had to suffer in order to reach spiritual rapture. Grandfather said that in many cases it was the spiritual leaders that used hardship and suffering as a way of keeping the common masses away from the truth so that the leader's religious power and prowess would not be challenged.

Part II of this book explains how Grandfather brought Rick and me to the understanding of the basic and simple truth that he set forth. No matter what he tried to teach, and no matter how simple he kept it, we always went on to try to complicate that teaching. He would constantly warn us that we were trying too hard. Also, once we mastered something we would then try and bring into it our religious crutches and toys, thereby complicating it. I guess that at times it was frustrating to Grandfather, but he never showed it in his teaching. He always maintained the patience of a saint. He was, however, a coyote teacher in that he would give us just enough information and then allow us to search for the final truth through trial and error. This way he knew that through our successes and mistakes we would learn things better. Yet always in the final analysis the simplicity of it all would win out.

7

Grandfather's Sacred Silence

One of the first things that Grandfather had to do was move us from the consciousness of modern society into the pure worlds of wilderness. Grandfather was not one to waste words or use long explanations. Instead, he would demonstrate by example what he wanted us to learn, or lead us to that lesson through something totally unrelated. One of the first lessons that I learned from Grandfather took place on the first day that I met him. Like all of his coyote teachings, that first lesson in the ways of the spirit had such far-reaching implications that it spans all time. Even today I still learn something important from that first lesson, and when I find myself doing something wrong or out of touch with the spiritual realities, it is because I have forgotten this first lesson. The lesson I learned was how to see.

Grandfather, Rick, and I had spent our first full day together. All the introductions had long since been over, and now Rick and I spent our time asking Grandfather many questions or listening to the stories of his wanderings. We were capti-

vated, riveted, to his every word. Grandfather never just told
a story through memory; he actually relived it. He had a way
of painting pictures with words so that the listener became
part of the story, feeling and seeing the same things that
Grandfather recounted in a real and personal way. I was most
interested in the stories of Grandfather's acute awareness and
how he seemed to be able to observe things that most people
would overlook. He seemed to have a different perception of
nature, a different consciousness. When we walked a short
distance together, he would pick out and show us countless
things that we had overlooked. I was absolutely captivated
by this ability and desperately wanted to do what he had so
easily done.

In a very sheepish way, mainly because I had just met
Grandfather and was afraid to ask, I asked him if he would
have the time to show me how he was able to see so much
so easily. He smiled at me and said, "Go to the edge of the
stream, seat yourself quietly, and look deeply into the land.
But it is also important that you look from deep within."
Without understanding what he meant by deeply, I wandered
over to the stream and sat down dutifully. I sat very quiet and
still, looking hard at the landscape surrounding the stream
and into the stream itself. I must have sat there for more than
an hour, but all I saw were a few passing fish, a small turtle,
and a handful of birds. I was beginning to grow exasperated
and bored at my lack of observation. This was nothing like
the short walk I had just taken with Grandfather where he
had pointed out so much to us.

Feeling like I had missed so much and also like a failure,
I decided to wander back to Grandfather's camp, thoroughly
disappointed with myself. Just as I arose to go back, I turned
to find Grandfather sitting just a few feet behind me. I was
so startled that I literally shook with surprise and sucked in
a panicked breath. He smiled broadly and motioned to me to
sit down beside him. He then began to show me what I had
missed. He pointed out the goings and comings of muskrat.
He pointed to a high tree where a raccoon quietly slept.
In another tree a screech owl was also sleeping peacefully,

appearing like part of the branch. He motioned to several nests, all of which had young. And in the distance he showed me where a doe and her fawn were feeding. This went on for over an hour, without a break. I was torn between speechless amazement and feeling a little stupid.

Finally Grandfather stopped pointing things out, more out of kindness than the fact that he ran out of things to show me. I asked him why he could see all of those things and I could not. He smiled at me kindly and said, "You look, young one, but you do not see. You look with the eyes of the White man and with the mind of society. In order to see these things, you must look with your spiritual mind, your pure mind, and see with the eyes of the wilderness. It is not your fault that you cannot see; it is because you have been trained to use your mind, and your mind cannot see the grand things of nature."

"But how can I learn to use this wilderness seeing?" I asked.

Grandfather answered, saying, "I have now only planted the seed inside of you. You will someday understand the purity of mind of which I speak." With that he left me to my thoughts.

It was almost six months later until I began to understand what Grandfather had meant by seeing with the pure mind. Several times during that following year he had talked about the pure mind, and several times he had said that the pure mind is also the spiritual mind, though still I could not really understand. I had heard Grandfather so often say that man was a duality, part flesh and part spirit. He had also alluded to the fact that modern man lives entirely in the flesh, and his spirit has become atrophied and weak at best. Yet I could not fully understand that pure mind or even how to get to it. Grandfather, as usual, was not giving any answers, only little clues. Little did I know that he was leading me to my eventual understanding of the pure mind. Looking back, I now realize that one could not teach another the concept of pure mind, only lead him there.

It was during my second Vision Quest that I learned the

powerful lesson of the pure mind. I had taken my first Vision
Quest within six weeks of when I first met Grandfather, and
now I stood at the verge of taking my second. At this point
I had known Grandfather barely six months but was now
beginning to understand the man and his ways intimately.
Though Grandfather said that my first Vision Quest was
very powerful, I felt that I had gained nothing of value,
except for a few insights into myself. Grandfather had said
this was because I refused to understand the Vision Quest
on spiritual terms. Instead, I was still looking at it through
the consciousness of the physical mind. Now at the verge of
my second Vision Quest, I thought that I understood enough
to make this one more productive, but Grandfather warned
differently.

The night before I left for my second Vision Quest, Grandfather sat me down and said, "You must learn to see and to
understand through the 'pure' mind, the spiritual mind. Going
into this Vision Quest or trying to understand the world of
nature with the physical mind in tow is to be blind, both
in flesh and spirit. You must learn to see things purely, for
only then can you fully understand the worlds of nature and
spirit." With those words I was off to my Vision Quest, full of
expectations, but also filled with self-doubt. I deeply feared
that this Quest would be the same as the first—one long and
torturous bout with boredom and self-doubt. As I wandered
to the chosen area, I wondered whether the Vision Quest was
really for me, or if I was worthy of any Vision at all. After
all, this was a sacred practice of the Native American, and
I was a White man.

The first two days of this second Vision Quest put me
through more hell than I had known on the first. My mind
would not shut down, I was horribly bored and uncomfortable, and I desperately wanted to leave. However, leaving
was out of the question, for I did not want to lose face
or endure the possible ridicule and disappointment of Rick or
Grandfather. After all, Rick had gone through his second
Vision Quest just a few days before, apparently with ease.
I was in hell. Deep into the second night, I awoke time

and again in fitful sleep. Each time I awoke, I was more determined to leave the Vision Quest and return to camp. At this point I couldn't care less about what anyone thought or the self-ridicule I would impose upon myself for being so weak. Upon my last awakening, I decided that I would swallow my pride and leave in the morning.

I awoke to a gorgeous sunrise. Nature seemed more active and intense than I could remember. Everything seemed to dance and move to the rhythms of the land. As I began to gather my few things in preparation to leave the Quest, I began to think about what Grandfather had told me just before I left. The words *pure mind* began to hammer at my heart, so much so that I forgot what I was doing. I had no idea as to what Grandfather had meant by this *pure mind*, but I suspected that the secret must lie somewhere within what he had said. Forgetting about the Vision Quest, I began to wander about the landscape, fully engrossed in the meaning of the pure mind. I did not know how long I had wandered, but a considerable amount of time had passed by. I so struggled with the thoughts of the pure mind that I was unconscious of everything else, even where I was.

I eventually arrived at a quiet pond quite close to the camp swim area, and there sat down to think. I gazed into the quiet waters of the pond, still thinking about what Grandfather had meant by the pure mind. The water was so still that there was a crystal-clear reflection of the sky and all that surrounded the pond. The reflection was so perfect that it looked as if I were looking into a mirror. Then a light breeze stirred the surface of the pond, and the once clear image shattered into a thousand pieces, then suddenly was gone. No reflection remained, just the troubled surface of the water. Then suddenly the word *thoughts* hammered into my head, and I jumped up in utter surprise and triumph. I finally understood what Grandfather had meant by pure mind. I was so amazed, so overwhelmed, that tears of joy filled my eyes.

The lesson of pure mind was shown to me by the clear waters. The pure mind was like the surface of a quiet pond, where all things were reflected purely. Once the logical mind sends in thoughts, analysis, definitions, qualifiers, and distractions, the image of the pond's quiet surface is disrupted, and the clear image of nature's reflection is destroyed. I understood then that in order to see into the worlds of nature, and ultimately spirit, as Grandfather did, I had to possess that pure mind. All distractions of the logical thinking mind would only produce an obscurity or destroy that pure image altogether. At that instant of enlightenment, I realized that I was no longer in the Vision Quest area and hurried back. As far as I was concerned, I was given a very powerful and profound Vision. The remaining time in the Quest area I would spend trying to fully understand what I had learned.

At the end of the fourth day of the Vision Quest I could not wait to get back to Grandfather and tell him what I had learned. I was so excited when I returned to camp that I virtually shook. Grandfather did not give me time to even speak, but immediately said, "So, Grandson, you have finally learned the wisdom of the pure mind. The pure mind is the spirit mind. It is that which opens us to the spirit of nature and most of all to the spirit worlds. It is our other mind. As I have so often told you, man is a duality of flesh and spirit. Man thus has a physical mind which only knows the things of the flesh, and man has a spirit mind that dwells in the realms outside the flesh. You have now touched that spirit mind, and it is through the quiet waters of the spirit mind that all spiritual communication will come. Any time the physical mind is present, the communications of the spirit are at best obscure or do not come through to us at all. So then, this pure mind, the spiritual mind, must be nurtured and grow as strong as the physical mind. Eventually, for those who wish to walk the spiritual paths of life, the spirit mind must become the dominant mind."

Awaiting no reply, Grandfather continued, "You have learned the wisdom of the spiritual mind, the pure mind, but you have yet to learn how to understand that mind and how to use it to communicate. It is through this pure mind that you will hear the voices of nature and spirit, and it is through this mind that you will send your voice to these worlds. But first you must understand these worlds beyond the flesh. For if you do not understand them, you will not know where you are going or how to get there. Once the pure mind is understood, you must then understand and master the vehicle, the bridge, between flesh and spirit. You must know how to make that journey between your prisons of flesh to the vast domains which lie beyond. What then remains is for you to understand these worlds, know how to get to them at will, know how to communicate with them, and finally know how to work in them."

"But what are these worlds and where do they exist?" I asked.

Grandfather said, "Man is like an island, a circle within circles. Man is separated from these outer circles by his mind, his beliefs, and the limitations put upon him by a life away from the Earth. The circle of man, the island of self, is the place of logic, the 'I,' the ego, and the physical self. That is the island that man has chosen to live within today, and in doing so he has created a prison for himself. The walls of the island prison are thick, made up of doubts, logic, and lack of belief. His isolation from his greater circles of self is suffocating and prevents him from seeing life clearly and purely. It is a world of ignorance where the flesh is the only reality, the only god."

Grandfather continued, "Beyond man's island of ego, his prison, lies the world of the spirit-that-moves-in-all-things, the force that is found in all things. It is a world that communicates to all entities of Creation and touches the Creator. It is a circle of life that houses all man's instinct, his deepest memory, his power to control his body and mind, and a bridge that helps man transcend flesh. It is a world that expands man's universe and helps him to fuse himself to the earth. Most of all, it is a world that brings man to his higher self and to spiritual rapture.

"There is a circle, an island, beyond the circle of the life force: the world of the spirit. Man lives also in this world, for his spirit walks also in this land in the spirit. Here man finds the duality in self, where at one moment he walks in flesh, and then again in spirit. It is a world of the unseen and eternal, where life and death, time and place, are a myth. A place where all things are possible. A place where man transcends self and fuses with all things of Earth and spirit. It is a place closest to the Creator and to the limitless powers of Creation. Beyond this place is the consciousness of all things, the final circle of power before the Creator.

"Man living in the island of self is living but a small part of what life is all about. Man must transcend the barriers, the prison of ego and thought, and reach the Creator. All islands, all circles, must be bridged. Each world must be understood, then finally fused into an absolute and pure 'oneness.' Then there can be no inner or outer dimension, no separation of self, just a pure oneness where man is at once all things. It is in this fusion of worlds that man will know all things and live the deeper meanings of life. Man moves within all things, and all things move within man. Then, and only then, can man ever hope to touch God.

"Modern man cannot know these worlds, these circles, that exist beyond his own ego. The logical mind will never allow man to expand beyond the ego or the flesh, for that is where the logical mind feels safe. Modern thought is the prison of the soul and stands between man and his spiritual mind. The logical mind cannot know absolute faith, nor can it know pure thought, for logic feeds upon logic and does not accept things that cannot be known and proved by flesh. Thus man has created a prison for himself and his spirit, because he lacks belief and purity of thought. Faith needs no proof nor logic, yet man needs proof before he can have faith. Man then has created a cycle which cannot be broken, for if proof is needed, there can be no faith."

I then thought long and hard about what Grandfather had said. I could only vaguely understand what he was telling me, but my most pressing questions were as to how one could get to these worlds beyond flesh, and how to function there. Grandfather, as usual, knew my questions before they were even asked, and said, "The pure mind is one of the common truths of all religions, philosophies, and beliefs throughout the world, Grandson. Only when man can reach the state of pure mind can he ever hope to come close to spiritual things, and ultimately to God. So the pure mind, the spiritual consciousness is the starting point. The problem today is that modern man does not know how to reach that pure mind. Instead, the dominant physical mind at best allows him only a brief and obscure view of the world of the spirit. That view remains tainted and ineffective. That is why modern man has devised all manner of complicated doctrine and ceremony to set aside his dominant logical mind and open his spiritual mind. But as always, these complications only heighten his confusion and distort any communication.

"There is a bridge, a vehicle, which I call the 'Sacred Silence,' that not only brings one to the ultimate purity of the spiritual mind and opens a clear communication, but also transports one to those worlds beyond the island of flesh. It is this Sacred Silence that sets aside all things of the physical mind and flesh, and enables us to live in and function in the realms beyond flesh. The pure mind is a common truth to all philosophies and religions, so the Sacred Silence becomes common ground. But it is in the approach and execution of the Sacred Silence where we find the major differences in all of those philosophies, religions, and beliefs. This, which I call the Sacred Silence, is found in all philosophies, though it is called by another name. That name is meditation. And in one form or another, surrounded by all manner of complications, it remains basically the same. It was once and for all the vehicle, the bridge, and the common ground.

"However," Grandfather continued, "meditation in the many centuries passed has become far too complicated and distorted. It is no longer the vehicle, but has become the end result. It is no longer dynamic and moving, but sedentary and ineffective. Yes, using the various forms of meditation will take a person to the worlds beyond the flesh, but that is all it can do. Man cannot live there, work there, nor is it a reality. It becomes a way of looking into these worlds in a very ineffective and distorted way and not knowing what is communicated. So, too, with the complications of modern forms of meditation, is the pure mind lost to the complications of the vehicle. The modern meditations, being an end result and very sedentary, cannot be used every moment of every day. Even if man reaches to those outer worlds, through the end result of his modern meditation, he cannot stay, but must come back to flesh reality.

"If you were to study any meditation," Grandfather then said, "you would find that it consists of four basic elements. First there must be comfort, and second there must be physical and mental relaxation. Then there must be a passive attitude, so that no outside distractions will interfere with the meditation. Finally there must be an absolute concentration point, that which focuses the physical mind in such a way that it ultimately disappears and allows the purity of the spiritual mind to become clear and dominant." At this point Grandfather related to me the story of the demon and the hair. Upon hearing that story, I could finally see why so many of the religions in the world, though trying to attain the same thing, had so many differences. It was because they used different hairs, such as ceremony, cathedrals, drumming, dancing, and all manner of other things that all were used as that "hair." It all began to make sense, for now I could see why man tried to complicate the obvious and simple. As man moved to a life of complication, his methodology of attaining that ultimate and pure meditation also became complicated, and eventually impossible. That is why meditation became an end result, for it was the complications that distorted the vehicle and ultimately the truth.

Grandfather then went on to explain his form of meditation, that of the Sacred Silence, which was to him and ultimately to me the simplest and purest form. The Sacred Silence is the vehicle that it was meant to be. Grandfather said, "The Sacred Silence is simple and pure. There is no complication, and thus it remains a dynamic and moving vehicle. There need be no religious crutches, toys, or 'hairs,' for these are found within us, and thus we do not have to rely on anything external. The first two elements of meditation, that of comfort and relaxation, are relative to one's beliefs.

Man does not need to be lying down or seated to be comfortable and relaxed. Are you not comfortable and relaxed when walking, when playing, or when talking? So, too, if you concentrate on nature and ultimately on the purity of your own mind, then you need not a passive attitude, nor any religious crutch or toy other than your own spiritual mind. So then, unlike the ineffective meditations of modern man, the Sacred Silence is dynamic and moving, usable every moment of every day. It also becomes a vehicle which takes us to the worlds beyond flesh and allows us to live there always, without struggle. It brings us to the duality of flesh and spirit, that ultimate oneness."

At this point I wanted to learn the Sacred Silence more than I can remember wanting anything else in my life. Yet Grandfather in his wisdom of such things wanted the seed to take root before he would go on and teach us the way, the vehicle. Several weeks had passed since our first conversation about the worlds of man and the Sacred Silence. My knowledge and understanding of these worlds grew with each passing day. I could now understand clearly that living in the prison of flesh was something that we had to transcend and never go back to. We had to arrive at the world of the spirit-that-moves-through-all-things and dwell there. From that new place, the real place that man belonged, we would then be able to move from world to world as the situation dictated. Then one day, without any prompting from me, Grandfather took us to the Sacred Silence.

Rick and I did not understand what Grandfather was doing at first. Both Rick and I assumed that it was another lesson in awareness, but what we found in the end was a vast new reality. Grandfather took us to the Sacred Silence by first moving us to a place of pure mind, that which we had practiced often, and now had become second nature to us. He then had us walk as the foxes do, in a slow and deliberate cadence, allowing all tension to drop away and seep from our body. We then fixed our gaze to the distant landscape using extreme peripheral vision, while keeping our minds free of all thoughts. Suddenly and miraculously the physical reality of the landscape began to shift slightly and it looked fresh and new. We began to see and experience things that we never before had seen. The whole of creation seemed to be in direct communication with us, and the spirit of the Earth fused with our very soul. We even began to detect things moving outside our physical realm of senses. Just outside our perception, we began to detect a world that had no physical counterpart, as moving and dynamic as physical nature itself, but vastly different—it was the world of spirit. We were both shocked beyond words, for this new world was so beautiful that we wept openly.

That was just the starting point. Over the years Grandfather taught us how to function in these worlds beyond self. He taught us to communicate with the world of nature and spirit as we could communicate with another person in the flesh. We learned to take journeys of the spirit and explore the vast spiritual domains that lie outside the reach of modern man. We created miracles, understood beyond words, and began to walk the line between flesh and spirit on a constant and daily basis despite the many distractions of the flesh and man. In the final analysis it all seemed so easy. We could not understand why man had done nothing but complicate and in so doing kept this wisdom forever out of reach. We finally entered Grandfather's world.

What was best of all was that Grandfather did not have to prove anything to us. By living in these worlds and proving for ourselves firsthand that everything Grandfather had said about these worlds was true, we had arrived at the best proof ever. It is one thing to see someone perform a miracle or talk about it, but that leaves one with the thought that the person who performed the miracle must be gifted in some way. But to actually do it myself and incorporate this miracle into my life, I needed no logical explanation or scientific proof. I knew that it worked for me whether I could explain it or not. It was real.

8

Inner Vision

Rick and I had practiced the vehicle of the Sacred Silence for many months before Grandfather moved on to teach us more. He wanted to make sure that we understood exactly what we were doing, and that we were experiencing the profound results of his worlds, the islands of man. After the many months that had passed and the frequent trips into these worlds, I gained a full understanding of each of them and could enter those worlds as I pleased, as long as the situation dictated. I finally could understand why Grandfather never wanted us to enter or live within the prisons of the world of self. In that world, we could plainly see that man was not really alive, but living in a vacuum, cut off from all that lies beyond. In this prison of modern man's mind and flesh, there was but only flesh, and life could never be full, real, and complete.

So too did I understand the world of the spirit-that-moves-in-all-things, the life force. Here we found that truly this is where man was supposed to dwell, the true and pure state of consciousness. In this world of the force we became part of the world of nature and understood its voices. We could better understand and control our bodies, and dwell in close harmony with the spirit-that-moves-in-all-things. Here we became part of nature and nature part of us, so that there was no inner or outer dimension, no separation of self, just that which Grandfather called a oneness of consciousness. We knew, when dwelling in this world, that nature and we were of one mind and one heart. We were truly children of the Earth in a real and dynamic way.

We learned, too, of the world of spirit, where we could exist there, and how to understand the laws of the spirit world. We understood that in this world was a vast domain of spirits. Some had physical counterparts that were connected to the world of flesh reality, but there were far more spiritual entities that had no physical connection or base. These were the spirits of the unseen and eternal, a vast domain so different than we had ever imagined. It was a world that fascinated us, yet at the same time terrified us, for we did not fully understand its power. We were children entering a world of the unknown, frightened, yet intrigued and curious. Over the months of searching, however, Grandfather would never allow us to go to the world beyond the spirit, for he said that this was the world of the shaman and we must fully understand it before we could enter this world.

Then one day many months after he had taught us the basic Sacred Silence, Grandfather went on to teach us more. At the time we could not believe that there could possibly be any more. The worlds of the Sacred Silence seemed more than enough, more than we could ever handle, far less understand. Then Grandfather sat us down and posed a question that really made us think. He said, "You now are beginning to understand the worlds of man that lie outside of the flesh and the prisons of the mind, but all you can do at this moment is look at these worlds. You are struck by the wonder of them all, yet you do not know how to listen to their voices or even understand what they are trying to communicate to you. When you enter these worlds, you are but a visitor. You do not understand how to communicate with them, nor do they communicate to you. You see them, but you do not understand.

"Now what I must teach you is how to listen to and understand these worlds of nature and spirit, so that you no longer look upon them as if through a door. Unless you can open this door, this veil, walk through it, and understand, then you will forever be outside of this world and separate. You must learn to become part of that world and function in its power. Simply, you have arrived there, but you do not understand how to speak to it or understand it when it speaks to you. Unless you understand the language and can communicate your desires, the spiritual world will remain forever out of reach, forever a mystery. The first concept you must learn is to know how to listen to the world of spirit and ultimately understand."

Grandfather was right. We had visited these worlds beyond the flesh but could not function there or communicate with them. It was like looking at these realms as one would look through the glass of a fish tank. Though we could see the fish moving and existing in their world of water, we were not in that world, for we were only in our own element and still removed. Only by entering the water could we become part of that world, and only by learning the language of the fish could we ever hope to understand what they were trying to convey to us. It was obvious that this communication was severely lacking. We could no longer be satisfied with just being in these worlds, but had to learn to communicate. Otherwise, the Sacred Silence would only be an end result, like every other form of meditation. We had to make the Sacred Silence dynamic and reciprocal in order for it to become dynamic.

The questions that we had to ask Grandfather were obvious: How do we learn to communicate with these worlds beyond the self, and what language is used? So many times I had heard Grandfather say that the world of nature and spirit does not understand the tongues of man, only the language of the heart. But what is that language of the heart? Surely, I thought, the heart's language must be universal, for all people of the Earth can understand the voices of Earth and spirit. I knew right away that this language could not be in the words of man, or defined in any terms of the logical mind. This language must be of a deeper and more universal nature, a concept that is known by everyone. But what could that concept, that language be? This was the problem that I had been struggling with for such a long time. For me, it was not enough to get to these outer worlds and realms of man. I had to actually communicate with them in a real way.

Looking back now, I can see why Grandfather had waited so long to teach us this dynamic communication. Grandfather wanted to make sure that we could use the bridge, or vehicle, of Sacred Silence easily and effectively. He wanted us to arrive at these places beyond the flesh and logical mind and see for ourselves the splendid realities that were missing in most people's lives. So, too, did he want us to develop an overwhelming desire to communicate with these worlds, and bring Rick and me to a point where we absolutely needed to communicate with them. We had to understand for ourselves that just getting to these worlds was not enough. There had to be more, much more. Even during the many times that we had asked Grandfather about the potential of communication and understanding, his answers at best were very vague. He would simply tell us that we were not ready, for even if we knew how to communicate we would never fully understand. The information conveyed to us would be incomprehensible, unusable, and therefore would subsequently confuse us.

I began to wonder about this communication that Grandfather so often spoke of. If this language was not in words, then what kind of language must it be? In a way, I began to imagine all manner of complicated communications. I wondered if the communications and languages were in dances, chants, songs, ceremonies, or traditions, or if they were in some heavy and complicated religious practice such as the Vision Quest. Then again I remembered that so often Grandfather would speak of the simplicity and would subsequently discount all of those complications. Although I tried, I could not come up with any usable or understandable form of communication. I suspected then that this communication was so simple that I was literally overlooking it through my lust to complicate and communicate. I finally arrived at the conclusion that it must be this simple, for Grandfather had said it was so simple and free for all people.

Then one night while sitting around our campfire, Grandfather revealed to us the awesome simplicity of it all. It was all so simple that I actually felt stupid for not realizing it before. He said, "The worlds beyond man, the island of the spirit-that-moves-in-all-things, the world of the spirit, and the realm of the shaman, do not speak to us in the tongues of man, but only through the tongues of the heart. These worlds know no words or logical concepts, but deal in languages that can only be fully conveyed through the heart. First we must arrive at these worlds and await their communications, and then we must wait openly and purely, with a mind free of all logical thought. For it is only through the pure mind, the spiritual mind, that we can ever hope to understand these conversations."

I could clearly understand what Grandfather was saying. In order to communicate and eventually understand, we had to go to the place where the communication originated. I could also understand that there had to be the pure or spiritual mind, the still waters, where nothing of the logical mind could interfere with that communication, like mental words. After all, the voices of nature and spirit would not filter through a mind that was in a turmoil of thought. The distraction of the words of the mind would only distort the truth. But the question still remained as to how these communications would reach us, and ultimately how we could ever hope to understand them. Grandfather then said, "To communicate with the world of man we must listen and understand with our physical mind, but to understand the language of the worlds of Earth and spirit we must listen with the purity of our spiritual mind."

"But," I said to Grandfather, "the spiritual mind and the voices of the Earth do not understand nor do they speak in the tongues of man, as you have so often told us."

"Yes, Grandson, you are right," he said, "they speak to us through a different language. A language that has been known for all time, yet a language that has been imprisoned and obscured by the dominant logical mind, which modern man nurtures and cherishes as their god. Yes, the language of the spirit and of nature is just as powerful and understandable as the words of man, but it comes to us in a different way." Grandfather continued, "It is the language of Vision, dreams, signs, symbols, emotions, and feelings. It is because of the dominance of the logical mind that this language has been set aside, buried deep inside of us, and imprisoned. Whenever it does surface, the logical mind is quick to crush it and set it aside as being childish rambling. It becomes our quest then to purify this language and make it dominant in our lives once again, so that it, too, has the same power and impact as does our logical mind."

As Grandfather's words trailed off into the silence of the night, I thought about all the times I had these feelings he spoke of, and how I set them aside as childish. So, too, could I remember so many teachers discounted these deep feelings in their students. Society in general does not give much credibility to these inner voices and whenever possible ridicules those who bring them to light. What I found out now is that these voices are every bit as real and even more powerful than those words and concepts that modern man considers the only acceptable communication. Now Grandfather was telling me that these Visions, dreams, signs, symbols, emotions, and feelings were real, acceptable, and in most cases more powerful and true than the words of man. For some reason I felt so good, for I had been chastised and ridiculed all of my life by teachers and society for relying on what I called my "gut feeling," now only to find out that I had been right all of this time.

I then recalled something that had happened to my father that illustrated to me the importance of following the "Inner Vision." When we were young, we were relatively poor. I remember my father working nearly sixteen hours a day in a local family-owned laundry business. I remember him coming home exhausted, pouring with sweat from the hot machinery he had to work with all day at the laundry. I rarely saw him during the week, for his work schedule was long and hard. At best he was home for dinner, then more often than not, back to work again. The financial aspect of all of that work was hardly rewarding. Sometimes he would not get paid for many weeks, and even when he did get paid, it was barely enough to keep us above a poverty level. As a child, I just could not understand this concept, working so hard, yet barely able to afford food. In comparison, pure survival was easygoing, like living in the Garden of Eden. I wondered how anyone could choose working in factories over living in the purity and simplicity of wilderness.

All of that aside, I remember the evening that my dad and mom had a long discussion at the dinner table, over something I could not understand at the time. My father had told my mother that someone he knew from "the business" had offered him a partnership. My dad said that to buy this partnership would take all of the money they had, and they would probably have to remortgage the house. I could see the anguish on my mother's face as my dad spoke, especially when my dad told her that most people felt that this new business venture would probably fail. That would mean my dad could lose everything if he invested in the partnership. Though they did not argue about it, they discussed it well into the night. My mother did not think that it was a good idea, and my father wanted to take the chance. They had a dilemma that could not be broken.

Finally, the next day at breakfast, my mom and dad began to talk about the partnership purchase again. They both agreed now that it was not worth the big risk, because there was such a good chance that the business would probably fail. However, the last thing my dad said to my mom before he left for work was that he was going to turn the deal down, but his intuition was telling him to buy into the new business. I clearly remember him saying, "Intuition is telling me to buy into it," and that stuck in my mind for a long time. Looking back at it now that Grandfather had told us how "Inner Vision"

worked, I knew that my father also had Inner Vision that day
of the decision not to go into partnership. As it turned out,
if my dad had bought into that partnership, he would have
worked only a year, then probably retired for the rest of his
life. The man who did eventually buy in made millions of
dollars in just a few years.

I told Grandfather this story and he said, "This intuition is
a form of Inner Vision that your father did not act upon. You
see, Grandson, this society you live in does not condone that
type of thinking or feeling. Everyone had told your father that
he should not go into the new business because it would most
probably fail. But somewhere deep in your father, he knew
that this would be the chance of a lifetime, and it felt right to
him. This feeling of intuition he had was right, but his logical
mind had crushed it and set it aside. He listened to his logical
mind instead of his heart. However, your father was right in
his decision because he could not really trust his intuition. In
order to be trusted, intuition must come to him through the
pure and spiritual mind; otherwise, it becomes distorted, and
many times interpreted wrongly. That is why modern society
looks down on the use of intuition, for in the final analysis it
cannot really be trusted with the logical mind as a filter."

Grandfather then warned us sternly, saying, "The Inner
Vision should not be used for self gain, for that is a step
to the 'dark side of the spirit.' Inner Vision should only be
used for things outside of yourself, where there is no self-gain
involved. You should never even think of asking Inner Vision
for answers that involve the self, only for things that will help
others and our Earth Mother. If the spirit world or the world
of the spirit-that-moves-in-all-things needs to communicate
to you on a personal level for your personal good, then it must
come from those worlds. It cannot come from your personal
request. Where the self is involved there is no clarity in
communication, and there is a tendency for evil. However, if
a communication comes unexpectedly and unasked for, and
it subsequently benefits you, then it is good."

This was a hard concept for us to understand at the time. It
was hard for me to understand how and when to use the Inner

Vision. If we could not use the language of Inner Vision for the self, then how could we possibly learn anything? After all, was it not through Visions, dreams, signs, symbols, and feelings, the essence of Inner Vision, that all knowledge comes? Is not the seeking of knowledge actually for the self? That is when Grandfather suddenly said, as if reading my thoughts, "Inner Vision is our teacher, and when we look at knowledge, it can be observed in two ways. If that knowledge is kept only for ourself and self-glorification, then it is of bad medicine, but if the knowledge is shared and used to help others, then it is of good medicine. It is then in the way that you ask this Inner Vision, and your ultimate motives, that will determine its power."

The first lessons in communication were very important to me, for now I was beginning to fully enter the worlds beyond flesh. I could now understand that communications come through Visions, dreams, signs, symbols, feelings, and intuitions, the language of Inner Vision. But I was perplexed, for this seemed to be a one-way street. The outer worlds could communicate with us, but we had no way of really communicating with the outer worlds. We were there, we could understand, but we could not communicate what we needed. I knew that we had learned but half the answer, and I also knew that Grandfather would not reveal more until we had mastered the Inner Vision. That was his way, and we dared not ask for more until we were ready.

9

Metamorphosis of Power

Nothing more was taught about the world of spirit for the next several months. Grandfather would not even give us a hint as to anything more. Instead, he seemed to be waiting for something to happen, not an external event but for something to shift deep inside of us. As I look back now, I can understand his hesitation teaching us more than we could handle. He wanted to make sure we could understand fully the secrets of Inner Vision and how to listen to the spiritual voices of nature and the world of spirit, and to become adept at communicating with our Inner Vision so that we could undertake the next step without restriction or confusion. He wanted us to first form the obvious question within our consciousness and then need the answer. There was no use for him giving us an answer to a question we did not fully understand.

For the next several months, Rick and I worked on our Inner Vision. We found first that there must be a quieting of the logical, physical mind for any communications to reach us. The Inner Vision could not be filtered through any logical thought, for the logical mind would only distort that communication if in fact any were noticed and received in the first place. It was an immense struggle at first to try and reach the purity of the mind, where there were no thoughts. It was a struggle that lasted many weeks, with only intermittent purity. We just could not understand the pure mind that Grandfather so often spoke of. It would not be until the middle of my second Vision Quest that I would understand that which Grandfather wanted us to achieve.

I was preparing for my second Vision Quest when Grandfather sat me down and told me how I should really prepare. I had finished my first Vision Quest several months before and I was eagerly looking forward to the second, but, paradoxically, I was worried I would get nothing from this second Quest. As far as I was concerned, my first Vision Quest did not reveal any grand Visions as Grandfather had so often spoken of, just little but important insights. Though Grandfather had said that my first Vision Quest was very powerful, I was not so inclined to agree with him, because of a lack of any real spiritual encounter. What I was looking for was a grand Vision, despite the fact that Grandfather had told me that it is in the little things where the grand Visions appear.

Grandfather told me that I had far too many expectations of this Vision Quest. I should go to it without expectations of any kind and remain open to the many little things that would come my way. I listened to what he said but, in my own way, refused to let go of my expectations, or fears. Simply I expected a grand Vision, but I feared that the second Quest would be much like the first. Grandfather also told me, just before I left for the Quest, that I needed belief and a "pure mind" before I could understand any Vision, big or small. I could certainly understand what Grandfather had meant when he spoke of belief, but I was not sure as to what he meant by the "pure mind." This, at the time, seemed rather unimportant to me as I wandered off to my Quest area.

The first day in the Quest area was a living hell. In what seemed to be no time at all, I was right back to the boredom and pain of the first Quest, as if there had been no break between the first and second. It did not take me long to become exasperated and angry. The misery of this Quest began to hammer at my mind. I was so often torn between leaving and staying, finally resolving myself to remaining in the Quest area for the four days regardless if I ever got a Vision or not. In a way, I somehow wanted to punish myself. It was as if there were two distinct people, two minds, living in my body. The one part wanted to teach the other part a great lesson through torture and denial. What I had failed to understand at the time was that I was beginning to identify the two places of existence, one of flesh and one of spirit.

During the second day of the Quest, my pain and frustration did not get any better, but grew steadily worse. Here, too, I could feel the ever-increasing sense that there were two selves. It became obvious to me that part of me did not want to be in this Vision Quest and the other part wanted desperately to stay. It seemed at times that one and the other were in direct conflict, almost an internal argument. However, it always seemed to be that one self of flesh was stronger and more verbal, while the other just seemed to communicate through the power of Inner Vision. One would nag at me to go, and the other would just give me the good feeling to stay and see the Quest through. It was such a conflict that I could not clearly make a choice. As the Quest progressed, the self that wanted to stay grew stronger and began to overshadow the other self.

Even though the bouts of wanting to leave lessened quite a bit by the end of the second day, I still had the nagging self-doubt and internal dialogue of wanting to leave. Though it was not as strong as it had been, whenever self-doubt crept into my mind, it seemed to make me want to leave even more. Then the other self would return and overwhelm me with the beauty of nature, the power of the Quest, and the need to stay and complete the Quest. By the evening of the second day, I again began to think about the fact that for the past two days I had been given absolutely nothing in the way of a Vision, far less even the slightest insight into all that surrounded me. For the entire evening and well into the night, I again struggled with the feelings of wanting to leave. This conflict followed me right into sleep.

I awoke on the third day with a sense of wonder, almost an excited anticipation that something was going to happen. However, after facing a few hours of the all-too-familiar monotony, I lost all hope and was pushed back to the desperate feelings of the day before. That is when I began to fall into a deep thought about all that Grandfather had told me. I ruminated about what he said of my first Vision Quest, what he had warned me of expectation, of belief, and most of all of the "purity of mind." I could easily understand all else. I realized that my expectations were standing in the way of the visionary insights. I could understand belief and faith all too well, but I could not understand what Grandfather had meant by the pure mind. The concept of pure mind lay beyond my grasp of understanding, but I began to sense its importance.

My mind began to become so caught up in the concept of the pure mind and its apparent importance that I forgot all about the Vision Quest. I began to wander almost unconsciously through the landscape, now totally unaware of where I was going or what I was doing. I never even thought of the Vision Quest, but was too saturated with my thoughts of the pure mind. Now its importance became even more important, for I could think of nothing else. Yet, important or not, it hammered at my mind and allowed me to think of nothing else. I eventually ended up sitting next to a small quiet pond, adjacent to our camp swim area. I sat there for several hours, pondering the questions of the pure mind. Yet I still did not have any answers nor did I yet realize that I had wandered away from the Quest area.

I gazed into the quiet surface of the waters for a long time, reveling in the perfect reflection of the surrounding landscape and sky. Then suddenly the surface was stirred by a breeze which jarred the once perfect reflection into thousands of images, then finally shattered it to obscurity. All that was left was the turbulence of the surface. Suddenly, out of nowhere, the word *thoughts* came into my mind. It was like I had been hit by a bolt of lightning. I finally understood what Grandfather had meant by the pure mind. The pure mind was like the surface of a quiet pond, where nature was perfectly reflected. The obscurity happened only when that quiet surface was distorted with the winds of logical thought. It became immediately apparent to me that this pure mind was what Grandfather had wanted us to achieve. For it was through the quiet waters of the pure mind that the communications with earth and spirit would come, purely, and without restriction or analysis.

As soon as this revelation struck me, I realized that I was away from my Quest area. I worried all the way back that I had broken some ancient law of the Quest and would be subsequently punished by either Grandfather or the spirits. However, I was so filled with the joy of finding such a grand answer that it overshadowed all worry and fretting. As far as I was concerned, this was a greater gift than any Vision I could ever hope for. I had learned such a powerful lesson and had been given a tremendous understanding of the power of pure mind. I was eager to return to the Quest area and search out the deepest meanings and ramifications of what I had just discovered. I was so overjoyed that I literally bounded back to the Quest.

As I settled back into my Quest, I began to fully understand what had been given to me. I realized that it is the power of the pure mind that makes all spiritual communication pure and unrestricted. The logical mind I viewed as a barrier or filter to that communication. Any time that logical mind became active with its need to analyze, define, verbalize, or interpret in any way, it sets aside and imprisons the pure mind. As I sat contemplating this, I began to realize a deeper sense of duality. I could now understand that the pure mind and the logical mind were almost two separate entities. When one was active, the other was sleeping or set aside. So, too, did I begin to understand why the logical mind was so dominant and strangling. After all, it was that mind that society wanted us to nourish. It was that mind that was like a spoiled stepchild, fed constantly by society, thus overshadowing and smothering the spiritual mind.

After my return from the Vision Quest, Grandfather seemed more than delighted that I had received the Vision of purity. It seemed to be what he was waiting for. Without question, Grandfather spent the next several weeks teaching me the deeper meanings and usage of the pure mind. I found that I could use this pure mind even when walking, and soon even as I held conversation with people. As the days passed by, my pure mind became stronger and purer. Now more than ever, I felt that there were two distinct selves, two places of existence, and definitely two minds. At once there was the physical body and logical mind, yet so, too, was there the spiritual body and mind, which began to reach a place of equality. It seemed Grandfather's sole ambition in his teaching to strengthen this spiritual existence.

I found that along with this purity of mind, or spiritual mind, as Grandfather called it, there came a stronger and purer communication with the world of nature and spirit. As the days passed, I could not only discern the grander communications from the outer worlds, but also the more subtle or hidden communications. Even these subtle communications were very clear and their meanings profound. After a while I could switch my consciousness at will. At once I could view things through my physical mind and body, and in the blink of an eye I could then see through the spiritual mind and body. Each day the sense of duality of self grew stronger, more defined, and purer. Along with this purification of the mind came the strengthening of the Inner Vision, to a point where the Inner Vision became as important as any thought.

As the days passed I began to feel the void again in my communication with the world of nature and spirit. It became painfully apparent that the Inner Vision was a one-way street. I could clearly hear and feel the calling of the spirit, but I could not speak to that world. I began to grow very frustrated because there was so much I wanted to convey, so many questions I wanted to ask. Even though Grandfather was aware of my frustration and the many questions that were left unanswered, he still persisted in developing the purity of my spiritual mind. I sensed he wanted me to reach a certain level of purity before he would go on. I realized the purity of the mind was more important than I had originally suspected.

Finally, one morning when I least expected it, Grandfather sat me down and told me of the communication between the flesh and the spirit. He said, "You have learned the power of the Sacred Silence. You now understand that Sacred Silence is a bridge or doorway to the world of nature and spirit. It is dynamic, not sedentary. Unlike the meditations of man and his religions where it is only an end result, the Sacred Silence is dynamic and a clear path to outer worlds of nature and spirit. So, too, have you learned of the powers of Inner Vision. It is through our dreams, visions, signs, symbols, and feelings that Inner Vision communicates to us. Now you understand to intensify and empower the Sacred Silence and Inner Vision, you must use the pure mind, the spiritual mind, so that you come from that place of purity.

"Now I must teach you how to convey your feelings, questions, and communications to the world of nature and spirit," Grandfather continued. "Like the language of Inner Vision, we must communicate to the Earth and spirit in the same way. The world of nature and spirit does not understand the tongues of man, but only the language of the heart. We must communicate with these worlds the way these worlds communicate to us, through Inner Vision. We must convey our needs, questions, and desires through the language of visions, dreams, signs, symbols, and feelings. This is the only way to make known to these outer worlds our needs. No other language can be understood."

I was consumed in thought over what Grandfather was telling me. I fully understood how the world of nature and spirit communicated to us, but how could we use these same visions, dreams, signs, symbols, and feelings in the same dynamic way? I could not understand how these things could be used. After all, in visions and feelings, there are no words. Up to this point I could not understand how these things could be controlled. I could certainly understand the concept, but I could see no way to bring it under control. So, too, I was excited and open to the concept, but also felt that it would be very complicated. I could not conceive the language of our hearts. Vision, after all, was something that seemed to be beyond our control.

Grandfather, as usual, anticipated my next question, and said, "You have been struggling with the question of how to communicate with the worlds of nature and spirit ever since you learned the power of Inner Vision. You began to grow frustrated because you could only listen and see, but could not communicate to those outer worlds. This frustration created a complication because you tried all manner of communication which never worked. All of this time the answer was sitting before you clearly and simply. You understood the way these realms of spirit communicated to you, but you overlooked the fact that you must communicate back to these worlds in the same way. Your confusion led to more complication and ultimately to your frustration."

Grandfather continued, saying, "You began to view your physical, logical mind as an enemy and allowed it to stand between you and the ultimate purity of the spiritual mind. You must not look at it in this way anymore. We all need our logical mind. The problem with man today is the logical mind is all that is nurtured and understood. Thus the physical, logical mind becomes dominant and suppresses all that is spiritual. It is not the mind's fault, but what society has trained it to do. What you must realize is that the physical mind is at once your greatest enemy and your greatest ally. You are not trying to destroy the physical mind when you seek the purity, only to set it aside and allow the spirit mind time to speak. After all, it is the power of your logical mind which guided you first to seek the things of the spirit. It is the logical mind which began your search."

Grandfather paused for a moment to allow his words to take shape and also for questions to form within me. He went on, "You see, Grandson, your logical mind is only an enemy when it stands in the way of the spirit mind. We are not seeking to destroy or diminish the power of the physical mind, but to get it under control. It must not dominate, but become part of the whole. Man is a duality, part flesh and part spirit. When the spiritual mind and the physical mind become equal, then it is what we call the 'Sacred Oneness.' Then we become one with flesh and spirit. At once we walk and understand in flesh and at the same time in spirit. So we should seek the equality of minds, not the destruction of one in favor of the other. So, too, it is the power of our physical mind which initiates and empowers the communications to the spirit world."

For the first time in a long time, I began to get a clarity in direction and in what Grandfather wanted me to accomplish. Up to this point, I had been considering the logical mind my enemy and fighting it every step of the way. I could not understand why I was getting the feeling of two separate selves. This feeling did not come from the destruction of the logical mind but from the illumination of the spiritual mind. A sense of great relief washed over me when Grandfather had said that we should seek to get the logical mind under control so that we could find an equality of logical mind and spiritual mind. The frustration was now set aside, not only because I had a very clear perception of where I was going, but also I did not have to beat and destroy my logical mind. In the past, try as I may, I could never beat the logical, physical mind, and it had become a source of much of my frustration. At least now I could use it as a valued ally.

I still could not understand, however, the concept of communication that Grandfather was intimating. There still remained the confusion over how a Vision was reversed and used by the logical mind, ultimately to be sent to the spiritual and natural worlds. This was the last remaining bit of information I needed, and up until this point Grandfather had only intimated the process, mostly skirting the issue. Certainly I understood what Grandfather was saying, but he was definitely and purposely leaving something out. That something was the way to communicate. At the time I suspected he just wanted to make sure that we had a firm understanding of the basics. Still it did not help me beat the frustration, as I yearned deeply for answers.

Again, before I could ask any questions, Grandfather said, "You are an example of what modern man has done for many years. You tend to complicate and overlook the simplicity of it all. The answer you are seeking is so simple, yet you are trying too hard to find the answers. The act of using waking visions, dreams, signs, symbols, and feelings to communicate with the worlds of spirit is as simple as using your imagination. If you can see the picture in your mind, make the picture vivid and real. When it becomes so real that you are actually in the picture, participating, then the power is sent to the outer worlds. It is the vivid reality of the picture you hold in your mind and the absolute belief that empowers it in the spirit world. There it becomes reality. What is physically manifest soon becomes spiritually manifest, and what is spiritually manifest soon becomes physically manifest."

I was struck speechless. It was all so simple, so simple that I had overlooked it for all of these months. It was as simple as holding a picture in my mind and believing it to be real. This simplicity I could hardly believe. I figured all along that there had to be much more complication, much more of a struggle in contacting the world of spirit or the world of the spirit-that-moves-in-all-things. Grandfather must have seen the dumbfounded expression on my face. I was struggling with a question that had not yet formed and I began to mumble something unclearly. The words just spilled forth and made no sense, making us both laugh long and hard. Here I was again, I thought, doing what I do best, complicating the simplest question.

As soon as we both stopped laughing, Grandfather said, "Yes, it is far more than just the use of your imagination or putting any picture in your mind. You must be directed to do so by Inner Vision and then to believe without a doubt what you hold in your mind is true. Your mental picture must be directed, commanded from Inner Vision. You then create a picture that is so real, so vivid, that you become part of that picture. It is so very real that you are there. This, Grandson, may sound easy, but it will take much practice to create that kind of image. This image is called visualization by many, but visualization is not enough. I believe that it should be called envisioning, for only envisioning can become real. The skill of envisioning and the absolute belief necessary to empower the envisioning have been lost to modern man. Yet at one time long ago, the envisioning was part of all beliefs and all religions.

"It is not enough to see it in your mind. It must be so real that you can not separate it from the world of reality. Yet this is still not enough. Just becoming part of envisioning does not give it the power necessary to send it to the world of nature or spirit, nor will it create any change in the world of flesh. You must first be directed by pure Inner Vision to be able to envision, and empowerment only occurs with absolute belief. Then it must be sent with a pure mind, the spiritual mind. Most of all, what you envision cannot be in any way selfish, but must benefit all of mankind and the Earth. So, too, you must never take credit for that which you have envisioned and have made manifest in the world of flesh. It is not by your power, but by the power of the spirit world that miracles occur. You are but a bridge, a vessel of that power, not the power."

I could clearly understand now what Grandfather was telling me. At once the power of envisioning became clear, but it was not as simple as I first thought. Now I could clearly see where the complications lay. Envisioning something would be difficult enough, even after being directed to do so by Inner Vision. But absolute belief would be more difficult, for belief is one of the most powerful forces on Earth and in spirit. I got the feeling that it would be many years before I could even perfect any envisioning, at least the envisioning Grandfather spoke of, and more years still to achieve absolute belief. I could clearly understand now why this practice had been abandoned by many spiritual seekers. It would take a lifelong commitment, a setting aside of self, to achieve this kind of purity. Yet at least now I was given a starting point, and I would dedicate myself to that Quest no matter how long it would take or how many failures I encountered.

As I continued to think about Grandfather's words and set them to paper, he said, "Take heart, Grandson, it is not such a long and difficult road to travel. Even in the beginning there are miracles. It is only man's logical mind that tries to complicate. If you can set aside the desperation, the need to complicate, then in this simplicity you will see miracles in every step of your journey. You do not have to wait until you reach some distant goal, for the power of envisioning and belief will be made manifest to you in every step of the way. Now go and begin your Quest, but keep it pure and simple."

PART THREE

THE
WAY

It is now that I want to set forth the basic philosophy and teachings of Grandfather. In the previous chapters of this book I wanted to teach the reader how Grandfather had arrived at this simple and pure truth, and in turn describe how he taught me. It is now my ambition to pass this along to you, in much the same way as in my basic Philosophy Workshop. Certainly, I would prefer to teach you face to face in that I know it would be much easier. Yet if you are diligent in your efforts and do not stray from the simplicity, then you will be able to learn. However, there is no way that the mere written word can ever hope to replace a physical class. My big fear is that after mastering the techniques that I teach, you may try to complicate them in some way. With complication you will be polluting the truth that Grandfather had tried for so long to simplify. Just accept the fact that these things are simple and obtainable by everyone. These things are everyone's birthright, a gift from the Creator.

If you look at the overall teachings found so far in this book, you will find that it comes down to just a few certain truths. First is the truth of the physical mind and body and the spiritual mind and body. Grandfather taught that man is a duality, part flesh, but also equal part spirit. He contended that anything done in the world of flesh was also done in the world of spirit and vice versa. Grandfather was quick to point out that our physical mind was at once our greatest enemy and our greatest ally. After all, it was the overtrained physical mind, the flesh, which obscured the spiritual mind. He did not seek to destroy the physical mind, but to make it equal. It is the physical mind that helps us become part of the vehicle which gets us to the power of the spirit.

Grandfather taught us that the Sacred Silence meditation was the cornerstone of all religions, philosophies, and beliefs of the world. It was through meditation that man could attain the spiritual consciousness. But now, in modern times, meditation has become an end result. Meditation, that which Grandfather preferred to call the Sacred Silence, was to be a bridge, a vehicle, the consciousness of nature and spirit. It was a way of setting aside the flesh and the physical mind and opening a channel of communication. To Grandfather, any meditation had to be dynamic, moving, and highly usable no matter what the person was doing. It had to be pure and effortless, so that a spiritual seeker could enter any world at will.

Inner Vision was the voice of nature, spirit, and even the Great Spirit. This was at one time common to all religions and beliefs of the world, but as man moved away to the complication of the physical mind, he lost touch with Inner Vision. The physical mind began to stir the pure waters of mind and distort all communication that was beyond the physical mind. In the struggle to dominate the spiritual mind, Inner Vision was obscured and in many cases shunned by society. People no longer paid attention to their deepest inner voices, but rather turned up the yammering voices of their logical mind. He taught us that Inner Vision could only be heard when the waters of the mind were quiet, thus reflecting the perfect image of spirit.

Finally Grandfather taught us the power of envisioning. Where Inner Vision was the voice of nature and spirit, envisioning was the vehicle of our voice, to communicate our desires and our need to these worlds. He taught us that it was not enough to envision what we wished to communicate, but we had to have absolute faith, pure mind, and Inner Vision direction to give that voice power. Most of all we could not do these things for ourselves, but for all things. He made it apparent to us that this envisioning process at one time or another was common to all, but like meditation and Inner Vision, this, too, was lost to the flesh.

What follows is a simple step-by-step approach to these pure truths. It is best if you just keep them simple. So, too, is it best to have a friend join with you in the following exercises and techniques. It is nearly impossible to do them on your own. Yet it can be done, if you are diligent. However, a friend can provide you with feedback and a much needed system of proof. Your successes can be freely discussed, and each of you will become a vital part of the other's success. Most of all, try and take these teachings one step at a time. There is no need to rush, for rushing is only trying, and the sheer act of trying negates itself. Fully understand each step and practice before moving to another. As always, there is the danger of complication if you take on too many things at once.

Unfortunately I cannot teach these things to you in the exact same way that Grandfather had taught me. You must remember that Grandfather and I were together for over ten years, so time was certainly on our side. Even in my classes this cannot be done. Again time is a factor. However, throughout nearly fourteen years of teaching I have been able to arrive at techniques that work well, and work for everyone, despite the factor of time. These teaching techniques, similar to Grandfather's, arrive at the same result. The only major change is that I leave a lot up to you to practice, and I rely heavily on your practice. Without diligent practice, these teachings will not work well. I also expect you to have an open mind, and try them, before you discount them. Remember that faith is a big factor in these teachings.

Whenever possible, I describe to the reader how Grandfather had taught me. This will give the reader an idea of where and how I arrived at my abridged method to fit the modern student. Sometimes you may want to shift from my method to Grandfather's or use a little of both. That is fine if it works for you. However, you must try both methods before modifying them to fit your personal learning style. Remember its dynamic and reproducible results will verify your ability to communicate. I know from the results of thousands of students that have gone through my Philosophy Workshop classes that these techniques will work and produce nothing less than miracles. All you need is faith and diligence in your practice.

10

The Sacred Silence

Grandfather did not like to use the word *meditation*. He felt that meditation, in the context that it is used today, was far too sedentary and an end result. He found in his study and wanderings that most meditations he observed were very limited or totally ineffective. They would take the practitioner of that meditation to the spiritual consciousness, but that is all they could do. In fact, he observed, these meditations could not be used in a dynamic, moving way. Most of them require the meditator to lie or sit comfortably, and when the deeper levels of meditation were reached, the meditator would be nearly comatose. Though Grandfather would be the first to admit that meditation, in some form or other, was used in every great philosophy and religion of the world. Meditation was a common thread.

Grandfather used the term *Sacred Silence* to define his method. He felt that the Sacred Silence was a dynamic form of meditation, where the practitioner could be active and thus use it in his daily life. After all, what good was a meditation if one could only use it in a sedentary and relaxed position? Grandfather was also quick to point out that the Sacred Silence was not an end result, but a vehicle, a bridge, to the outer realms of man. It was not enough to use the Sacred Silence just to get to the spirit world; we had to function there. The Sacred Silence in turn would lead one to discover his duality, where one becomes part flesh and part spirit. In his everyday activity the practitioner of the Sacred Silence could view the world through the physical senses and then with a shift in consciousness could view the world through spiritual senses and spiritual mind. Eventually the practitioner would become "one" with both worlds, fusing them together.

Even though there are no major differences between meditation and the Sacred Silence, the slight differences that are evident only mean they must be taught in a different way. Where one is very sedentary, the other is dynamic, moving, and highly usable in everyday life. Thus the approach and teaching of the Sacred Silence is done in a different way. Though at first it begins in a rather sedentary and relaxed physical condition, it quickly transcends into a dynamic meditation. With daily practice the reader can move in a meditation within the first two weeks of practice. Eventually the reader will be able to talk and fully function while holding on to that meditation. Not only will the reader arrive at the world of the spirit but will be able to function easily there.

Grandfather's Islands of Man

What I first must do is to make it clear to the reader what Grandfather meant by the islands of man. Grandfather said that there were four worlds of man. The world of the "Living Dead" is where mankind today is imprisoned. It is a world of flesh, of logical thought, where the flesh is the only reality, the only god. He said that modern man could not escape from this prison of flesh. Not because he did not know how to but because that is where the physical mind feels safe. In the beginning, he contended, man was of two minds: a physical mind and a spiritual mind. Because modern society constantly feeds the physical mind and does nothing for the spiritual mind, the physical mind becomes dominant and the spiritual mind all but atrophies. So, too, the physical mind does not want to give up any power, so any time a slight spiritual thought arises, the logical mind crushes and obscures it or ignores it altogether.

So it is the flesh and the physical mind that imprisons man in this land of the living dead. Mankind cannot escape this world because he lacks spiritual knowledge and direction. What's more, the realms of the spirit cannot be proven in modern terms of science and technology. The realms beyond the flesh and physical mind are based on faith, and the physical mind cannot know faith, for the physical mind needs proof before it can have faith. Thus mankind has created a cycle that cannot be broken, for if proof is needed there can be no faith. Further still, we as a society do nothing at all for the spiritual mind. Grandfather believed that modern religion was just worship and possessed no spiritual training. Thus, unless mankind could approach the world of spirit with absolute faith and had the spiritual training, then mankind would never transcend the prisons of flesh and the physical mind. Man would always yearn to be whole, and never achieve the greater self. Man living in the prison of flesh is not really living at all. He was encapsulated in his flesh and imprisoned by his physical mind. He could only then imagine a world of spirit and beyond, but he could not go there. Man's life in this world is sorely limited, suffocating, and horribly empty. Man was left yearning for answers to what life is all about. So, too, he is cut off from the forces of natures' spirit and the world of spirit. He becomes disillusioned, knowing that there should be more to life but not knowing what it is or how to get there. Mankind tries to reach a point of fulfillment through religions and philosophies that no longer work, desperately striving to find spirituality in complicated dogmas and myriad religious toys. His desperate searching leads him to nothing but dead ends. Man becomes saddened, empty, and cut off from the vast domains that lay forever outside the grasp of the physical mind.

Grandfather called the world that lay beyond man's prison of flesh the realm of the "spirit-that-moves-in-all-things" or the "force." Grandfather said that the world of the force was where man truly belonged and should live every day. He told us that we should abandon the world of the flesh and forever live in the realm of the spirit-that-moves-in-all-things, never returning to that prison of the flesh. Here in the realm of the force, mankind would become the duality of flesh and spirit. He would be in direct contact with his deeper self, his limitless mind, his true emotions, desires, and deepest memory. Here he would function dynamically and would understand the vast domains that lie outside the flesh, that which life is all about. Here, too, he would communicate freely with the spirit of nature, creation, and the worlds of the spirit in a real and dynamic way. This world was man's birthright, abandoned long ago by a society that worships the flesh.

Grandfather said that there was a world beyond the realm of the force, which he called the world of the spirit. It is in this world that we find our spiritual counterpart. Here we can touch the wisdom of the "unseen and eternal," all those spiritual beings that once lived. Here we find all knowledge of the past, and all of the possible futures. In this world which knows no time or place, nor any limitations of the flesh, we can create the miracles which will become manifest in the reality of flesh. Here we gain wisdom that cannot be known by the flesh or the physical mind, and here we draw close to the truth. Man knows no limitations or restrictions here. His spirit soars free of all worldly distractions, and his consciousness fuses with all things of flesh and spirit. Here mankind truly realizes the duality of self, where at once he walks in flesh and in spirit, and knows both worlds equally.

Beyond this world of the spirit, Grandfather said that there is the realm of the shaman. Grandfather considered the shaman as one who had transcended his religion and now walked a pure and simple path to enlightenment. A shaman was a practitioner of duality, where there were no impossibilities. A shaman was a light at the end of a rather long and dark tunnel of flesh, living always in both worlds. It was in this realm of the shaman that man could come close to the Creator. It was here that man could create miracles and transcend the trappings and prisons of the flesh. Grandfather believed that this was the world where all people should strive to be. To him, it was the ultimate purity and truth. Here the shaman would become a vital part of leading others to that path. He believed that the duality of flesh and spirit was the dynamic meaning of life.

Grandfather said that these four worlds were separated by veils and that the Sacred Silence was the bridge, or vehicle, that takes us through these veils and to the outer worlds. It was the Sacred Silence that set aside our physical mind and allowed the pure spiritual mind to emerge. So, too, was it the Sacred Silence that made the communication between flesh and spirit pure and unrestricted. It was in these worlds beyond the flesh that man was at his best, in absolute communication with all things of flesh and spirit. Here life was rich and full, not empty and full of pain, void of fretting, striving, and slaving of the flesh. It is into these islands beyond the flesh that the Sacred Silence will carry you, too. And it is through the Sacred Silence that you will learn to communicate and function in these worlds in a very real way.

Again, it is going to take faith, and faith is one of the most powerful forces on Earth and in spirit. It is not enough for me to just describe these worlds of man to you. You must live them. Grandfather just led us to these worlds, describing them in great detail for us. He told us exactly what we would experience and feel in these worlds, then left it up to us to find out for ourselves, as you will find it out for yourself. I cannot prove these things to you. You must therefore prove them to yourself. No one can prove anything to you, nor can anyone provide you with faith. This is up to you to decide through your own results. It is then that you will build your own belief system. Remember that these worlds will be proven to you in the little miracles that occur, and soon you will understand them to be reality.

The Four Basic Elements of Meditation

If you study meditation from any philosophy, religion, or belief system, you will soon discover that they all contain four basic elements. Grandfather said that meditations, in one form or another, were found in all philosophies and religions, and no matter how hidden, they were a common truth that bound all philosophies and religions together. After all, meditation is the vehicle that takes man from his physical consciousness and introduces him to the spiritual consciousness. Also, it is here in the practice of meditations that we find not only the great truth but the basic reasons why so many religions and philosophies differ. It is in the way that each religion arrives at the spiritual consciousness that makes them different. The tool of meditation remains constant.

The first basic element of meditation is that of relaxation. A person must be relaxed before he or she can embark on the journey of meditation. If the body is stressed out, or is trying too hard, then meditation cannot be achieved. If the body is not relaxed, then it creates a major distraction that must be transcended.

The second element of meditation is comfort. Here, as with relaxation, the body must be comfortable so that discomfort does not create a distraction to that meditation. Yet modern thinking dictates that comfort and relaxation must be achieved in a very sedentary way. Many believe that one must lie down or sit comfortably in order to meditate. I do not agree with this way of thinking, for relaxation and comfort are relative to one's belief. I am comfortable and relaxed when I talk, walk, play, or during any number of other active pursuits. I have learned to view comfort and relaxation in many ways. It is not achieved just through sitting or lying in a semiconscious condition.

It is with these first two elements of meditation, comfort and relaxation, which is my primary argument for body and mind control. The mind is an awesome tool to say the least. The powers of the mind, coupled with choice and belief, can create any reality. I hear many people say, "You are what you eat." I believe you are what you think. We have all heard expressions like: "The mind can make any situation a heaven or a living hell," or "One man's heaven is another man's hell." I can see this power acting on people every day in any situation. In severe conditions, torrid heat and humidity, abundant flies, and torturous accommodations, I can watch one of my students thoroughly engrossed in what he is learning while the student sitting right next to him is complaining, miserable, and swatting flies. Same situation, same conditions, but with far different choices.

So then it is body control which helps us to transcend conditions which others would consider to be miserable, uncomfortable, or tense. By choice, belief, and the powers of the mind, we can meditate under most if not all conditions, good or bad. The choice is up to us. By learning to control the body and mind, we learn to rise above the conditions which would prevent most people from entering the consciousness of meditation. Relaxation and comfort are relative and subjective, based on belief and choice. That is why in many beliefs, philosophies, and religions, the worship is done in rather relaxed and comfortable conditions. It is only when man seeks to show others that he has transcended the trappings of flesh that he will prove his ability by sitting naked on a glacier, walking hot coals, or bearing any other designed hardship. Most people believe these abilities are unattainable because, rightly so, they are extremes.

The third element needed for meditation is a passive attitude, or so people think. Essentially, this passive attitude is used when one tries to transcend distraction. As has been stated, the sheer act of trying negates itself. So a passive attitude is not trying, but just allowing distraction to pass through and away without any struggle. Let's say for instance that a person is beginning a meditation and a stray thought enters his head, pulling him away from the focal point of the meditation. If that person gives that stray thought power and tries to force it out of his mind, then the stray thought gains power and becomes difficult to remove. If, however, the stray thought is identified and passively removed from the mind, then it loses its power as a distraction and quickly disappears. Passive attitude is used most of the time to beat any distraction, whether mental, physical, or environmental.

However, I have found that the passive approach does not always work. Grandfather made us aware, almost immediately, that there were several methods of beating distraction. He said that there were three ways in which the "demon of distraction" could be beaten. Foremost was a passive attitude, allowing the distraction simply to pass. Sometimes the distraction had to be accepted by confronting and identifying that distraction and realizing your weaknesses. Other times the distraction had to be beaten back with a brutal aggression. At other times all three methods would have to be employed to successfully remove the distraction from the physical mind. Grandfather warned us that we should never allow the fighting of a distraction to become a distraction itself. I found that when the elements of comfort and relaxation are taken care of, then the only distraction comes from the mind. Yet, the more active a meditation becomes, the more distractions must be faced and controlled.

I have found that in most cases, the passive-attitude approach to beating a distraction works well. However, sometimes I must confront a distraction, such as when I must face a fear, real or imagined. A passive attitude will not work when facing a distraction such as fear, because it must be identified, then faced or confronted. When I deal with outside distractions of some force and magnitude, I find that I must beat these back with a brutal aggression. It is this aggression which breaks the law of passive attitude because in this case it is the only approach that will work. Especially dealing with severe conditions, when one's very survival is at stake, an aggressive fight will be necessary. Yet this aggressive fight is used the least.

Finally the last element of meditation is the "concentration point." When Grandfather met the old sage, Zee, he heard the story of the "hair," which is just another word for the concentration point. When the man handed the curled hair to the demon and asked him to straighten it, the demon was under control. These "hairs," or concentration points are the main differences in all the religions, beliefs, and philosophies of the world. There is a lavish assortment of hairs throughout the world: songs, chants, drumming, music, ceremonies, customs, traditions, religious objects, crystals, and countless others. Even the act of going to a place of worship is in fact a concentration point. For in every faith, religion, belief, and philosophy there are concentration points. Even within the religions that seem to follow the same belief, the concentration points are very different.

What Grandfather wanted us to do was to transcend all external concentration points. He considered them all to be self-limiting crutches, where mankind, without his religion's toys, would not be able to reach a spiritual consciousness. As man became more encapsulated in the flesh, the more complicated his concentration points became. So, too, does modern man further complicate by integrating concentration points from a religion with other religious concentration points. Mankind has to transcend all external concentration points, including his own religion, in order to walk the pure path of spiritual enlightenment. In man's desperate search for truth, he jumps from one religion to another, striving to find the easier method. In so doing, he does not climb to the top of the mountain but makes several starts only to abandon them and start over. He forever remains at the bottom of that mountain. I find that in many cases the concentration points become the religion itself. It has become painfully apparent that instead of believing in and worshiping the Creator, modern man believes in the religious leader and worships the doctrine.

Though Grandfather taught us first by using a rather sedentary approach to the Sacred Silence, the external concentration points were quickly replaced by internal concentration points and then abandoned altogether. As far as he was concerned, we were born into the world naked and that is the way that we should approach the world of spirit and the Creator. Man in the pure environment of nature, the only temple of creation, needs nothing. Everything else soon becomes a self-limiting crutch. Yet he understood fully that we needed some sort of crutch to mark our beginning. But this crutch, this concentration point, had to be easily broken and cast aside. To him, the best crutch was developed by our own mind, our greatest enemy and our greatest ally.

Journey to the Sacred Silence

When Grandfather began to teach us the method of using the bridge of the Sacred Silence, he kept the concentration points to a minimum. He had us lie down on a mossy bank next to a stream, and he would lightly drum as he told us what to do. It was rare that he would use the same beat; usually he changed the beat with each new journey into the Sacred Silence. He did not even want the drumming to become a concentration point by making it repetitious. Within a short period of time he abandoned the drumming altogether, and we would use the music of the stream or the winds as an aid to our concentration point. Even the sights and sounds of nature were quickly replaced by more internal concentration points. It was not long before the only concentration point that we used was wholly found in our own minds without any reliance on the externals. Finally even the concentration points in our minds were abandoned until we needed nothing to reach a pure Sacred Silence.

Grandfather did not allow us to stay in a lying position for long, either. The lying or sitting position would only breed a sedentary and unusable meditation. Instead, we began lying, and as the weeks passed, we would reach the Sacred Silence in a sitting position. As our abilities grew, we could walk in the meditation and then eventually run. It was not long before we could instantly trigger a meditation and reach the outer worlds regardless of what we were doing or what external circumstances surrounded us. Grandfather did not say that sedentary meditations were bad, but instead indicated it was but a half truth. He believed that one should use a sedentary meditation during periods of intense spiritual introspection, but also one should be able to achieve the same results no matter what the activity. Sedentary meditation is not good or bad, but just part of the overall process.

Entering the Sacred Silence

It is best to do these techniques with a willing partner, preferably someone who is also seeking the same path of spiritual enlightenment. One partner becomes active in the meditation while the other partner guides him through the meditation. Then roles are reversed. Approaching these techniques alone is a little more difficult and requires a slightly different technique. Also, at first, the partner that is guiding the Sacred Silence will become part of the concentration point which will aid in the meditation. This way, with the guiding commands of the partner, the mind is not likely to stray from the task at hand. However, as soon as possible, the need for a partner should be abandoned and soon replaced by the concentration point of one's own mind. If this is not done, then the partner's voice will become a "hair" for the meditator.

At the beginning stages of the Sacred Silence exercises, it is best for the meditator to lie down on a comfortable surface. This will be abandoned soon enough, but at first it is necessary until a more dynamic form of meditation is achieved. So, too, is it good to have some sort of background sound that will block out all other distracting sounds. You may wish to use the sounds of nature, or even a light drumming, as Grandfather used for me, but I find that it may be better to use a lighter New Age music. I find that this will produce better results at first, in that we all come from a very distracting world and need a stronger background music in the beginning. I suggest some kind of New Age music that tends to create a soothing atmosphere. I use Kitaro in the first few meditations I direct. This can be easily abandoned for the sound of light drumming, then for the sound of nature, as one grows stronger and more confident in the Sacred Silence. It should be noted that these things, too, will become a crutch if they are not outgrown and abandoned.

At this point all the meditator has to do is to lie down and relax, allowing his or her partner to guide the meditation. It is important at this point not to cross the hands or legs, but to lay flat out. If the lower back tends to ache in this position, then elevate the knees on a small pillow to alleviate the stress on the back. It is also important to realize that as one slips into meditation, the metabolism slows and the body will feel chilly. It is a good idea to put a light blanket over you. Even though this will feel a little warm at first, you will find that the body cools down quickly. This is especially important until you learn body and mind control and are able to warm the body and raise the metabolism at will. You should also choose a place that is quiet and otherwise free from all external distraction. I use the environment of my lecture hall for the first few meditations to achieve this quietude. Yet all of this will be abandoned soon enough.

Now it is the duty of your partner to guide you through these first several meditations. The guide, as I will now call your partner, should use a soft voice and otherwise remain as quiet as possible. It is the guide's duty to bring you into and out of the Sacred Silence meditation by controlling the music or drumming, and fully understanding what he or she is trying to achieve. Here, in the first stages of learning the Sacred Silence, the guide is of utmost importance and will remain important until the meditator can achieve the Sacred Silence on his own. From watching the progress of my students, I find that this can be done in anywhere from three to five meditation practices. Yet I have seen people who need no guide, and in other cases, the meditator needs the guide for many meditation exercises. Just remember that each of us is different. No matter how long it takes you to transcend the guide, we will all eventually arrive at the same place. Remember, too, that some people are better at one thing than at others. Some find it easy and some find it a little harder, depending on the individual. So give yourself a break from the all-too-familiar critic in your mind.

Once the meditator is lying down, comfortable and relaxed, and the background is filled with soft drumming or music, the guide begins the journey. The concentration point here will begin with the breathing, because as you will see, breathing will become instrumental in forming a "trigger," which I will explain later. At this point, as the guide, tell the meditator to concentrate fully on his breathing. Tell him to feel the rise and fall of his chest and the flow of the breath in and out of the lungs and across the lips. Remain silent for nearly a full minute while the meditator concentrates on breathing. It should be noted here that the guide should not start too quickly, for it will not allow the meditator to fully concentrate on breathing. Nor should the guide allow more than a full minute to pass, because with prolonged time the meditator may allow the mind to wander away from the breathing.

Now comes the time for the "command breaths." This sequence begins with the guide telling the meditator to take a deep breath, hold it for a few moments, then at the command of the guide releasing it completely. The guide tells the meditator that the next time the command breath is taken he should focus all distraction, tension, and discomfort into that breath and let it all go with the exhalation. Let everything flow out with the air leaving the lungs. Now repeat the command breath process about two to four more times. Each time the meditator should imagine and believe that all distraction is passed out of the body and mind with each exhalation. It is important to note here that the meditator should give his full attention to each facet of the Sacred Silence exercise, not only to build a firm foundation, but also to keep focused. Here the full concentration point is the breath and the subsequent exhalation of distraction.

Next, the guide leads the meditator through a "complete body relaxation" sequence. Here individual parts of the body are isolated. On command, the guide will tell the meditator to take a deep breath, hold it, flex the muscles, and tighten the isolated parts of the body. Release the flex with exhalation. Then tighten the muscles again, coupling them with all the distractions, and let it all go. The meditation sequence will allow the body to relax deeply, never removing concentration from that part of the body until the next part is announced. The meditator should not rush ahead, but follow the guide. I begin this relaxation sequence with the feet, ankles, shins, and calves, using those four parts as a single part. Then I move to the thighs, buttocks, and lower abdominal area, using those three as a whole. I then move to the upper abdominal, back, and chest, in unison. Then on to the shoulders, arms, forearms, and hands, treating them again as one part. Then finally the head, neck, and face. Finally, when all parts are covered with this tensing and relaxing sequence, I end by telling the meditator to take a deep breath, hold it, then tense the entire body. This time when the command is given to let go or give in, the entire body sinks deep into relaxation.

This sequence of intermittently tensing a part of the body, then relaxing it, accompanied with an exhalation, does a number of things. First it moves the full focus, the concentration point, of the meditator to his own body. Second, by tensing the body and tightening the muscles, then letting go of that tension, the body reaches a deeper state of physical relaxation. Third, and finally, the meditator is training himself to relax using the command breath. It is also important that the meditator not lift any body part away from the ground, floor, or lying surface, for when the tension is released, the body part will hit the ground and disrupt the meditation. So, too, is it important to let go of the tension completely, giving in fully to relaxation, and not fighting it in any way. Some may find that the neck is one of the most difficult areas to relax. If at any time a place refuses to relax, then just repeat the process again.

Now the guide will move on to the image of the "white light" sequence. This process now moves the concentration point away from the physical action of tensing a body part and subsequent breathing to that of a more internal nature. The guide will tell the meditator to imagine a column of pure white light coming down from the sky. (Remember that the eyes are closed throughout this meditation.) The guide will direct this light through the whole sequence by telling the meditator to feel it enter the toes, warming, soothing, relaxing, and healing. The light will then move to the feet, to the ankles, to the shins and calves, to the knees, thighs, buttocks, and lower abdominal areas. The guide should repeat the words *soothing, relaxing, warming,* and *healing* as the light moves up the body. The meditator should focus rapt attention on each facet of the process, pouring his full concentration into the light and all of its properties.

The light then moves on to fill the torso, back, chest, and upper abdominal area. Now direct the light over the shoulders and down into the arms and hands. Then move it to the neck, head, and face. Finally, when the entire body is filled with this light, it expands beyond the parameters of the flesh and fully encapsulates the entire body. The meditator should not only imagine the full warmth and relaxation, but also feel a deep sense of security and peace. What this sequence accomplishes is moving the concentration point away from all physical action and into a more internal state. It helps the meditator further concentrate on each body part, relaxing them further with the aid of the imagined light. It also creates a feeling of security and deep peace.

Now the guide should direct the meditator's concentration onto the body "position" sequence. The guide tells the meditator to direct his full attention to the position of his body, feeling how the body is lying and the position of each limb, head, and all other body parts. The guide should allow the meditator no longer than a minute to focus on body position.

The guide should then move to the "gravity" sequence. Ask the meditator to feel the heaviness of the body, being pulled to the Earth by the forces of gravity. The meditator imagines and feels the sensation that every part of his body is heavy, as if there is no skeletal support system. This part of the meditation further moves the concentration to the internal and further relaxes the body.

Now the guide asks the meditator to move to the "pain" sequence. Here the guide asks the meditator to focus attention on a particular pain or discomfort. Allowing a few moments to pass as the meditator isolates and identifies the place of pain, the guide now instructs the meditator to qualify the pain. The meditator will identify and qualify the pain or discomfort as throbbing, tight, burning, stabbing, etc., or any other combination of descriptions, but he must keep it simple. The guide then directs the meditator to give the pain a shape, and the meditator will imagine the shape to be geometric, like an octopus, amoeba, or any other imaginable shape. After a few moments of concentration on the shape, the guide asks the meditator to combine the shape and the description of the pain or discomfort visually in the mind.

It is at this point that the guide must be strong, almost demanding, so that the meditator thinks of nothing else. A firm but quiet voice is helpful for this sequence. Command the meditator to make the pain or discomfort round like a ball. Almost immediately, demand that the meditator make it smaller, smaller, smaller, concentrating on making the ball shrink. State that the pain is as small as a marble, and then tell the meditator to pass it out of his body completely, imagining that it disappears into the Earth. At this point there is a slight pause for no more than a moment, allowing time to be filled with the soft drumming, music, and focus of the meditator. The meditator's focus has been removed from the whole internal and is now on a specific location, a specific task.

Now the guide will ask the meditator to enter the soaring, flying, or "floating" sequence. It is important here to note that the guide must not let this sequence go on for more than a minute. The meditator's mind may wander because of the intense relaxation effect and possible joy of flying. Remember, there is a thin line between sleep and meditation, especially with the sedentary meditations. What the guide does now is to ask the meditator to imagine his body becoming lighter and lighter, until he imagines himself actually floating above the lying body. Ask the meditator to fly with the sound of the drumming or music, across imagined landscapes. The meditator's mind is focused on imagined externals and senses the freedom of flight. Here, also, the meditator will feel a great sense of peace and relaxation.

Now ask the meditator to go into the "trigger" sequence which I call the "breath to heart." Here the guide asks the meditator to return from flight and pay full attention to the guidance. The meditator is asked to take a deep but gentle breath and to hold it. Holding the breath, the meditator imagines the last shreds of tension, distraction, and pain to build in his chest along with the breath. Now the meditator is commanded to let the breath go easily and to keep exhaling until he can physically feel his heart beating in his chest. This sequence is then repeated two to three more times until the meditator can feel not only his heart beating, but his pulses in his wrists, thighs, neck, and even the blood tingling through his scalp.

Now the guide gently moves the meditator away from the Sacred Silence and into full consciousness. First he tells the meditator to stretch gently and move his hands and feet slightly. He then asks the meditator to move his arms and legs slightly, slowly moving to a full sitting position. The meditator must realize that at this point the body is deeply relaxed and going into a quick sitting or standing position may produce a certain dizziness or a light-headedness. The meditator may also find that he may keep this deep sense of relaxation for up to an hour after even his first meditation. So, too, he will sense an expansion in his awareness, but may not be able to fully explain. This is all normal. The guide and meditator should wait at least a half hour before reversing roles. This will give the guide a chance to relax and the meditator to come back to full physical consciousness.

On Pain

To your delight, you may find that you were able to pass pain out of your body for a moment or for a prolonged period of time. It may never have returned at all. Some of you may have passed away even chronic pain. This is of no surprise, for you have just realized a very powerful tool. What I tell my students is that if they were able to pass away the pain for even a fraction of a second, then they have succeeded. The only thing standing between a fraction of a second and an eternity is the limitations of their belief and the restrictions of the mind. They will soon be able to control all things in this way. Essentially, this pain sequence can be used for many things other than pain. It will work for self-doubt, fear, failure, or any other negativity. With things like self-doubt, fear, and the like, you have essentially qualified and identified them. All you now need to do is to give them a shape, make them round, and then pass them away.

Nearly all of my students are able to pass away pain or discomfort immediately. Some may only pass it away for a fraction of a second, while others can pass that pain, even chronic pain, away for several hours. There are many still who pass the pain away for good. After a little practice, most are able to pass the pain away and keep it away. Yet even the pain that returns to those few comes back less severe. I believe what is accomplished by the pain sequence is not the masking of pain, but actually a way of commanding the body to heal, or take care of, itself. It is not necessary for a meditator to know the healing mechanics or physiology of any healing process. Instead, this process is set in motion by the pain sequence. Many of my students will admit to accelerated healing time any time this pain process is instituted.

Most of my students have also used the pain sequence for getting rid of negative fears, or emotions, as well as performing some feat of body control. For example, one of my students, Sandy, had problems with fear of the dark. Every time she walked from the campfire to her shelter, she became almost paralyzed by intense, unfounded fear. One evening before leaving the camp area for the night, she imagined the fear as being a dark ugly spiderlike shape surrounding her heart. She poured her concentration into that fear and made it round, and then made it smaller and smaller, until she passed it out of her body. She walked nearly all the way back to her shelter without fear. When it did creep in, she immediately imagined the ball of fear passing out of her, and she was able to complete the journey with the same attitude she had when going there in full daylight.

Another one of my students, John, had an extremely difficult time walking the small log that is suspended across the swim area at camp. Even with extremely good balance this is no simple task, for the log is a few inches wide, and at the center point it is wobbly, smooth, and round. John could not take more than a few acrobatic steps without falling. Finally he decided to try the pain sequence method, only replacing the pain with his poor balance and image of falling. After sitting for a bit in quiet meditation and believing that he could walk the log, without a second thought he got up and crossed the log without falling. The combination of passing the possibility of failure from his mind, as he had learned to do with pain, and believing that he could do it easily worked successfully. He did just that.

The Trigger Sequence

Whether you know it or not, what you have succeeded in doing is to set in place a strong trigger which will instantly transport you to the Sacred Silence. That trigger is the "breath to heart" sequence. It commands your physical body and mind to let go of its grasp on the flesh and allow you to relax instantly into the Sacred Silence. With each time you practice the above meditation you will make the "breath to heart" trigger stronger and more dynamic. It will be there any time you need it. I suggest that you only use this trigger when it is absolutely necessary, for just using the trigger all the time begins to weaken the trigger. When I was younger, I only used it in times of dire need. So, too, did Grandfather warn us about using the trigger unless it was absolutely necessary. Yet each time we practiced any meditation we would further engrain the trigger.

When I first learned of this internal trigger of "breath to heart," I asked Grandfather why it was so important. He said, "The trigger is used when you need to enter the veils of the Sacred Silence without delay. It will immediately take you there. However, when you practice the Sacred Silence, go there using the way I have taught you. That way the trigger grows stronger. Never use any external triggers, for you may not be able to use them in times of need. Imagine if you learned to hold your hands in a certain way that would trigger the Sacred Silence. If then your hands were engaged in something else, then you could not use your trigger. That is why the trigger I taught you is internal."

The more I learn and understand the many ways that mankind uses triggers to meditate, the more I see the importance of making any such trigger internal. Simply, if outside circumstances do not allow you to get into that certain position, if you cannot see the trigger, or physically use the trigger, then you stay hopelessly wrapped in the coffin of the flesh. Even the "breath to heart" trigger will soon be transcended, and you will find that the only trigger you need is your will. The journey to the vehicle of Sacred Silence will then be governed and guided by your will and the spiritual mind alone. No other trigger, external or internal, will be necessary.

Now you can test your trigger and know that it works. The guide should have the meditator sit quietly in front of him. Holding and supporting the meditator's arm, the guide should place his fingers gently but firmly on the meditator's wrist. As the guide, you should now pay rapt attention to the meditator's pulse, its intensity and rate. A stopwatch will not be necessary, as the results are quite bold and startling.

Now tell the meditator to take a deep breath, hold it while gathering all his tensions in his chest, then command the meditator to go to his heart. At this you will find that the pulse drops, sometimes disappears altogether. It is not only a dramatic drop-off in beat but also the intensity of the pulse decreases. Repeat the process again with a "breath to heart" sequence, and you will find that the pulse drops off even further. This is a dramatic indicator that the meditator has locked into the trigger. A deep relaxation and meditation is the only thing that would cause the pulse to drop off that quickly and dramatically.

After you have a firm grasp on the Sacred Silence and your trigger becomes strong, you may want to practice a slightly different approach. Go through the "breath to heart" sequence with your partner and allow the trigger to bring you deep into the Sacred Silence. On the third cycle of "breath to heart," simply will your heart to rise above the point where you first began. Don't wonder how this will be accomplished, but rather will it and believe it can be done. Your guide will be shocked to discover that this time the pulse drops off as usual, but as soon as you will your heart rate up, it goes up, dramatically. Many of my students report that with diligent practice they can drop their heart rate to below 30 beats per minute, then in an instant catapult it up to 170 beats per minute. This is also the beginning of dynamic body and mind control.

Once you have gone through this basic meditation exercise, I suggest that you practice it once or twice a day for twenty minutes. You will not need a guide. Just follow the same sequence of events that your guide had taken you through and each time making the "breath to heart" sequence stronger. As you practice day in and day out, you will find that you begin to carry the sense of great peace and relaxation with you for longer and longer periods of time. The sense of expansion will also become a part of your life and after a short while follow you through the day. You will find a great sensitivity to things that you never before paid any attention to, and you will find your awareness expanding dramatically.

Basically, what you are doing is moving from the prison of flesh to the realm of the spirit-that-moves-in-all-things. It is in this realm that you will soon live always and fully.

Remember that the Sacred Silence is a vehicle, a bridge to the outer worlds, and not an end result. It is the way to set your physical mind aside and allow the spirit mind to come forth. It is also the way to purify all communication and function in the worlds outside the concept of flesh. The Sacred Silence—meditation—is a common denominator, a basic truth, which runs throughout all religions, beliefs, and philosophies no matter how badly it has become obscured by the countless "hairs." The more you practice the Sacred Silence, the stronger and purer it becomes, the more you become part of the worlds beyond the prison of the flesh.

11

Inner Vision Purified

Now that you have experienced the vehicle of the Sacred Silence, you have essentially arrived at the worlds beyond the prison of the flesh. Although you are there, you cannot easily function in these worlds other than to marvel at the experience. Now we must journey beyond the vehicle and learn to understand the communications from these worlds. We listen with our Inner Vision, for the worlds beyond flesh do not communicate in the words of man. Instead, these realms communicate through visions, dreams, signs, symbols, and feelings. Here I use *visions* not in the sense of the visions obtained in the Vision Quest, but in the context of waking dreams. In this chapter you will learn to listen to your Inner Vision and to purify it with the Sacred Silence. But first we must identify it, learn how to ask it a question, and how to receive answers.

Inner Vision is the true language of the deeper self, the spirits of nature, and of the spirit world. Grandfather believed that it was the very voice of the Creator, and I will have to fully agree with him. It is in essence all of these things, and

I have never found the "pure" Inner Vision to be wrong. I emphasize *pure*, because Inner Vision filtered through the pollution of the logical mind can give us obscure results and distort communication. In the logical mind's quest to dominate, it will destroy any communication from our spiritual mind, even falsify communication, in order to make us turn away from all quests for the spiritual mind. The dominant physical mind ensures its importance and remains unchallenged by making the spiritual mind obscure.

Many people have already encountered Inner Vision but in its most obscure form. They refer to it as a gut feeling, intuition, hunch, or by many other names. These are just weak and polluted forms of Inner Vision. No doubt you have experienced the "feeling" of being watched as you walked in the forest, or possibly around your own home. Possibly even in a town or city. Well, you probably were hearing the voice of Inner Vision, and I find this not the exception but the rule. If you had known how to use your Inner Vision, you would have known not only exactly what was watching you but also its location. Sometimes many of my students have told me that they had the feeling that something was wrong, or that someone needed them at home. Upon calling they found that they were in fact needed. Others have told me of times that they knew something bad was going to happen, even before it happened, only to find out that it happened shortly after they received the feeling. Many of us know police officers or military veterans who got the "hunch" not to enter a room or walk down a certain trail, only to find out that they would have been hurt or killed if they had not paid attention to their hunch and done so.

It is these hunches or feelings that are in essence the weak and distorted callings of the Inner Vision. Even though there is no way we could physically know something was about to happen, someone was watching us, or something was wrong with a certain trail or room, we got a clear message. These hunches and feelings are constantly happening to us, our friends, and to society in general, but they are wholly over-looked and unquestioned. The reason for this is that up until now the voices of Inner Vision are very vague, unreliable, and not understood. So, too, our physical mind is diligently at work crushing or hiding the weak messages and distorting the stronger ones. In fact, it is only the stronger ones that ever make it through the distraction of our physical minds. I believe that there is hardly a moment that goes by that we are not bombarded with all manner of communication from the worlds beyond flesh. If we could ever shut down our physical minds long enough, we would not have to wait very long for a communication.

There is an excellent way to teach people what the Inner Vision really is, how it answers, and how to ask it a question. My teaching method deals with something that everyone is familiar with: that of forgetting something but not knowing what it is. So often we go to the store to pick up a mental list of things and know full well that we are forgetting something. It is that "knowing" that is actually the Inner Vision trying to tell us what it was. Remember, Inner Vision does not only come from the worlds beyond the flesh, but it is also a direct link to our deeper physical selves. It communicates to all of our memory, our instinct, our primal self, our healing centers, and even to our body control centers. In fact, it is the Inner Vision that warns us of oncoming sickness or other ailments.

I find that using the situation of "forgetting something" to be an excellent way of teaching people the basics of Inner Vision because that feeling is well known and common to us all. I am going to tell you a story, and as you read, I want you to put yourself right into the story, imagining that it is really happening to you. The more you put yourself into the story, the better the results. In this story I am going to take the place of your deeper self, the place of all stored memory, just the way it would happen in real life. As you read the following story it is best done in a quiet place free of distraction so that you can fully concentrate. Many people find that by periodically closing their eyes and imagining themselves doing what I ask, it makes the "feeling" clearer.

Imagine that you are in your home packing for a long-awaited trip. It is getting close to the time that you are going to leave and you are packing the last remaining items. Feel the excitement over the trip welling up inside of you. Imagine now that you are closing your bags, zipping zippers, buckling buckles, snapping snaps, and pulling and cinching backpack belts. Pretend that it is some kind of camping trip to a distant place and you have saved and planned for more than a year. As you finish up the last of the packing, you are suddenly hit with the feeling that you are forgetting something. It is a funny feeling that seems to hit many of us at gut level. It is a feeling of something being at odds with yourself, a tension of sorts. Some of us sense it as an overall feeling that something is just not right.

Now you grab your packing list and look it over, mentally trying to remember if you packed each item as you go down the list. Satisfied that you have packed everything on the list, the feeling still gnaws at you, now in a more disturbing and intense way. As it grows closer to the time to leave, imagine yourself packing your bags into your vehicle. As the last one is packed, you get the feeling of forgetting something again. This time it is more demanding and apparent. It is the same feeling you get when you are shopping and feel that you are forgetting something from your mental list. Again you search your mind for answers, but with no results. The feeling nags and nags as you close up your home and prepare to leave. You may even check the list again to see if there is something you overlooked.

Finally you just give up in exasperation, lock up your home, and take off for the airport in your vehicle. The excitement over leaving for this long-awaited trip overcomes all feelings of forgetting something. As you drive, your mind is consumed with other things, the tension inside of you is now overlooked while the mind wanders over the trip itinerary. At the airport you park your car and carry your bags to the check-in counter. There, as your bags move along the conveyor belt and disappear behind a curtain, you are suddenly hit again with the uneasy feeling of forgetting something. This time the feeling is stronger than ever. It is more rapt and demanding, more tense and uneasy. You carry this feeling with you right onto the airplane.

You settle into your seat, and soon the door is closed. Now you're on your way, and the excitement for the trip returns and blocks out everything else. You can feel the plane taxi down the runway, then suddenly the engines roar and you are pushed back in your seat with the energy of the takeoff. The feelings of excitement for the trip are now compounded and exhilarated by the rush of adrenaline felt from the takeoff. You can feel the plane climbing along with your excitement. The long-awaited day has finally arrived. As the plane levels off and the excitement wanes, you begin to think about the overall trip and your plans. Your mind wanders back to your baggage, and suddenly the feeling of forgetting something returns boldly into the pit of your stomach.

This feeling of tension is stronger than before. Its nagging quality seems overwhelming and at once compelling. Compelling you to search your mind again for answers, but to no avail. As the plane levels out fully and the seat belt sign goes off, you resolve yourself to the fact that you cannot do anything about the forgotten object now. People begin to wander about, you hear the sound of papers shuffling, food being served, and excited voices now trailing off to a light din as they mix with the ever-present drone of the jet engines. You begin to settle in for the long flight, put your seat back, and grab a magazine from your bag. You reach up overhead to turn on the reading light. As you look toward the light, you suddenly realize that you have forgotten your flashlight!

The feeling of remembering the flashlight is so overwhelming that you let out a sigh of amazement. It feels like somehow you have unburdened yourself of some heavy internal load. The once tense feeling in the gut, the uneasy feeling of something at odds with itself, is suddenly let go, and your gut feels like it shifts. It is the all-too-familiar feeling of relief. You have felt it before as you shopped but could not remember one of the items on your long mental list. Soup, bread, carrots, potatoes, and, and, and? Soup, bread, carrots, potatoes, and, and, and . . . cereal! The internal tension and utter relief that follows upon remembering is very common and well known to us all. In essence, the tension felt when forgetting something is the calling of your Inner Vision trying to get your physical mind to remember. Your Inner Vision knows very well what you have forgotten, but it cannot convey this in the words of the physical consciousness. When you finally remember, your Inner Vision gives a sigh of relief and settles back to a place of equilibrium.

This inability for the Inner Vision to convey to the mind the item that you had forgotten becomes evident any time you search your mind for answers and come up with nothing. When you finally let go the actions of your probing physical mind during the plane flight, you reached up to turn on the light. The beam of light became a symbol that your subconscious mind picked up, and the symbol was sent to the logical mind, which suddenly remembered your forgotten flashlight. Thus, when your Inner Vision is trying to contact you, you get the feeling of uneasiness, tension, something at odds inside of you. When you find the correct answer needed, or satisfy the yearnings of the Inner Vision, there is the great feeling of relief that washes over you. This feeling of deep relief, the release of tension, is an indicator that you have satisfied your Inner Vision.

So here in the story of the forgotten flashlight, the Inner Vision was a combination of feelings and symbols. However, this is not the only way the answers may come. As stated before, the answers will also come in dreams, visions, and signs. The rarest kind of Inner Vision answer, it seems, comes in the form of signs. As far as I am concerned, signs are a very visionary and spiritual answer. For instance, let's say that you are walking in the woods and you come to a fork in the trail. You know that both trails will eventually lead to the same place, take the same amount of time to travel, have the same difficulty rating, and have splendid scenery. As you begin to take the right trail, you are confronted by a crow flying right at you, veering off only after it gets very close to your face. Somewhere deep inside you know it is a sign, a warning of some sort, so you take the other trail. Later you find out that a landslide occurred about the same time you would have been on the trail that was wiped out. You realize that the sign was sent from the outer world.

Inner Vision answers also come in waking visions and dreams. Both are treated here in about the same way. If you do not pay attention constantly to your Inner Vision, then Inner Vision will get to you eventually through your dreams. During sleep, the physical mind goes through periods of rest, and the spiritual mind sees it as an opportunity for contacting you. Certainly we are all bombarded with dreams every night. Some are unimportant and merely the physical mind's way of playing. These lack real meaning. However, dreams that remain with you after awakening, leaving you uneasy, and begging for attention are usually from the spiritual mind. If you do nothing to satisfy them, then they will return again and again if you do not act on them. I believe as Grandfather did, in that dreams are only impotent for those who do not keep in constant communication with their Inner Vision.

I warn my students constantly to avoid anyone who thinks that he can interpret your dreams. Maybe a long time ago when people lived in tightly knit cultures and possessed the same belief system could this be possible. But today it is impossible. To prove that to yourself, get ten people together that you know very well. Ask the group to picture a coiled snake in their minds. Now ask them to define the snake with a word, an emotion, a feeling, or a phrase. Ask them to hold that description in their minds. One at a time ask each of them to give you a word that describes their feelings for the coiled snake. You will get words like *fear*, *alertness*, *shiny*, *slippery*, *relaxed*, etc. Very rarely will you get two who will come close to the same meaning. That is because today symbology is personal. What something means to one person will not be the same for another. With this in mind then, how could anyone interpret a dream? If I dreamed a coiled snake, it would surely be different than your coiled snake. The same holds true for a vision.

If the calling of Inner Vision and the subsequent answering seems so simple to you, it is because it *is* very simple. The only complication comes when trying to purify Inner Vision and make it absolutely free of the polluting effects of the physical mind. What we just created in that little story of the forgotten flashlight was a way of teaching you the Inner Vision, but the story was not real. You created it and relived it in your mind. Your mind created the feeling. But this served its purpose of showing you the way of Inner Vision. The difference between pure Inner Vision and imagined Inner Vision is immense indeed. However, it is a long struggle to purify Inner Vision and know when the mind is not giving you a false reading. You certainly know how to purify Inner Vision already, and that is through the Sacred Silence.

I remember one of the first classes where I taught the students how to use Inner Vision. Ironically it was not during the Philosophy Workshop but on the Advanced Survival Class. The Philosophy Workshop classes did not exist at this time. Two of my students, Ben and Andy, were having trouble spotting animals. Yes, they had seen deer, raccoon, opossum, turkey, and several other species, but specifically they were having trouble seeing the more elusive animals, mink in particular. In fact, they had gone over seven days without seeing even one. At best they had seen tracks, but these were few and far between. The rest of the class had little trouble finding mink. Ben and Andy tried every kind of awareness device but still could not find any mink, and their frustration level was running quite high. Ben was so frustrated that he wanted to leave the class and go home. He was so down on himself that he felt that he just did not measure up to everyone else's ability.

I sat Ben and Andy down and took them through the Inner Vision exercise, using the exact same forgotten flashlight exercise I used here. I then asked them to stand up, close their eyes, and while facing a particular direction, I asked them to ask themselves in which direction was the nearest mink. Their gut tension became immediately apparent, indicating the direction they were facing was not the right one. They then returned and repeated the exercise and again were met with the tightness in their gut. Finally after several direction changes they felt a profound release in their guts. This was the Inner Vision telling them that they had located the exact direction. I then asked them to ask themselves how far away the nearest mink were, using the same technique. Again they went through the exercise, beginning with an area just a few feet in front of them and subsequently finding the release more than a hundred yards away.

Ironically, in their minds, they both had arrived at the same area independent of each other. This surprised them both to say the least. At first they would not believe the results of the exercise, mainly because they had both chosen an area where mink would not usually go. I told them to forget about what their logical minds were telling them and to go and see if their Inner Vision had been right. They both wandered to the distant area they had chosen. As they neared the exact location, they found a small seep and little swamp that they did not know existed. There on the distant bank was a rather large mink, feeding on a small fish. As they watched, several smaller mink, apparently her juvenile offspring, joined her and began to play with the fish on the bank. This play went on for the better part of an hour.

When Ben and Andy returned, they were both amazed at what they had done, and told me so. They realized the location of the mink was totally beyond their physical senses and in an area that they would have otherwise overlooked. Even though they had been in the camp area for more than a week they did not know the small swamp had been there. I simply told them that they had used their Inner Vision as a way of tapping into the spirit-that-moves-in-all-things. I could tell by their expressions that they did not really believe me, but in their minds I know there could be no other explanation for the results other than the possibility of a lucky guess. They subsequently used that technique for locating all manner of other animals and plants at greater distances throughout the remainder of the week. Each time they were met with the same startling results, and each time they came closer to understanding the power of Inner Vision.

As I have said, Inner Vision is a link to the world of the spirit-that-moves-in-all-things, which includes all entities of the Earth. The story of Ben and Andy and their encounter with the mink is repeated countless times by my students. But many ask if this is where the connection ends, assuming that it will only work with things that society considers living. Not so, for it extends beyond what we assume to be living, that of the flesh, and reaches out to all things of nature. To the Native American, all things of the Earth were considered living and possessing spirit. Rocks, water, sky, and all other things were part of the tapestry of the spirit-that-moves-in-all-things, the life force. As you will observe in the following story, one of many hundreds of such stories, the communication reaches well beyond what society deems as living.

Mike is a young and very successful entrepreneur from the Northeast. During his first Philosophy Workshop, he found out firsthand how the communication of Inner Vision reaches beyond the flesh, and to the very substance of the Earth. We had just completed the first Inner Vision exercise, and I had asked the class to go out and find the nearest animal. Not only were they to determine the exact location of that animal with the Inner Vision, but also the exact animal. As the class left the lecture hall, Mike stayed behind, apparently beginning his Inner Vision exercise in the lecture hall. It really baffled me to watch him, for instead of looking for animals in the distance, he was apparently searching the farm compound with his Inner Vision, such were his physical actions.

He exited the barn, and from my vantage point at the window, I watched him move across the snowy field. Without breaking stride he walked directly to the tree line, about a hundred yards from the barn. Without hesitation I watched him brush away the snow, pull out his knife, and dig down into the frozen ground. That action was a sure indicator that he was not looking for animals, as I had asked the rest of the class to do. I could clearly see him reach into the small hole and remove something, but I could not make out what it was. Apparently he had found what he was looking for because I heard his scream of joy right through the walls of the lecture hall. He danced around, skipping and rolling in the snow as he headed back to the barn. I watched him hug several other students, and his animations foretold his telling them of his success.

As he entered the lecture hall covered with snow, he was so beside himself that he could hardly speak to me. I told him to calm down and catch his breath. Subsequently he told me the story, barely able to believe what he had done. I on the other hand just took it for granted, for he had accomplished nothing that I hadn't witnessed in other students countless times before. Apparently he had been captivated by my lecture on arrowheads and other projectile points that I had delivered earlier on in the day. I had shown the class several old arrowheads and three spear points, all made out of flint. He had marveled at them, for in all of his wandering he had never found a full, undamaged projectile point, and apparently longed to do so. This yearning followed him right through and beyond my lecture and workshop and into his Inner Vision.

Unlike the rest of the class, who were asking their Inner Vision the exact location of an animal, he instead asked for the exact location of any projectile point. I had mentioned earlier that our farm sat on the site of an old Native American encampment, so he figured that this place would be ideal for his inner search. He went through the exact Inner Vision procedure as the rest of the class, but instead of searching for an animal, he searched for an arrowhead. When he first got the release, he could not believe it, but decided anyway to go exactly to the location where he imagined his Inner Vision had taken him. He walked directly across the cornfield, which was covered with four inches of snow, to the place beside the large old rock on the tree line, and dug down the three inches as his Inner Vision told him. There he found the projectile point he now held carefully in his hand.

It was exactly as his Inner Vision had told him. No searching, no digging of several test holes, no wandering around, but just the exact location. What he said was more amazing was that shortly after getting the "release," he knew exactly what the point would look like. It was over four inches long, perfectly formed and in perfect condition, and made of light-colored flint or chert. This did not surprise me, either, for it is the rule and not the exception to get the image of an object or animal shortly after the release of Inner Vision. He was able to achieve several more successes throughout the remaining days of the class, turning up four more projectile points, a grinding stone, and a well-shaped flint hoe blade. By the time he left the class, he was well above the 95 percent accuracy range. The only time he failed was when he allowed his logical, physical mind to come in and pollute the process.

Another story which is very common is the use of Inner Vision in spanning time and distance. Greg was an older fellow who was a student during one of my first Advanced Tracking and Nature Awareness classes. This was also one of the first classes in which I began teaching the use of Inner Vision. I took the class through the Inner Vision exercise and again told them to find the nearest animal, identify that animal, and identify its exact location. Like Mike, Greg had his own ideas. After the exercise Greg came up to me and asked me if I would take him out of camp so that he could make a phone call. His mannerisms told me that it had something to do with the Inner Vision exercise that we had just completed, and I suspected that the phone call was one of confirmation, such was his sheepish attitude.

After probing, he finally admitted that he had not done the exact exercise I had asked the class to do. Apparently he had lost his keys the day he left for the class and the missing keys were on his mind. Before he left he had looked feverishly for them because they were the keys to his file cabinets, his home, his car, and so many other things. He had heard me mention that Inner Vision reaches to our deepest memory, so he figured that his deepest memory might remember where he had left or lost the keys. He told me that in his mind, using his Inner Vision as a guide, he had searched his entire house with no clear results. But when he mentally searched his office, there was a release when he got to his personal desk. He just knew that the keys would be there, but he wanted to make sure so that he could have his secretary put them in a safe place.

I took him out of camp and to the nearest phone booth. I watched him from the front seat of my truck, and I could tell from his now deflated attitude that he had gotten some bad news. Returning to the truck, he told me the keys were not where his Inner Vision had told him they would be. His secretary had remembered seeing them on his desk at one point before he left the office, but they were not there now. I then asked him if he had gotten a full release from his Inner Vision, as strongly as he had when I went through the forgotten flashlight story. He thought for a moment and then told me that it was not as strong as it had been when I first gave the lecture. I then asked him to close his eyes and go back to his office, mentally going through the entire place.

He closed his eyes and remained absolutely motionless for a long time. Then suddenly he jolted awake and without a word left the truck and headed to the phone booth. I could almost imagine the reaction of his secretary to his subsequent request. I watched him talking on the phone, and his body seemed to become electrified as his jaw dropped in disbelief. He was shaking with delight as he reentered the truck. He told me that his secretary had found his keys exactly where he had been told they would be. He said that they were found in the drawer of a small lamp table in the corner of his office. Not only had his Inner Vision told him of the location, but it also told him that they would be in an old staple box in the back of the drawer. He said that at first he would not have believed the location because he never used that drawer, and he could not see why his keys would end up there.

He said that when the secretary had found them, she, too, was amazed, but he would not let on as to how he knew. As the secretary talked to him on the phone, the office cleaning man had walked in and heard them talking about the missing keys. He told the secretary that he had noticed the keys on the desk during cleaning and had put them in the lamp table drawer for safekeeping. It was hard for Greg to explain his way out of that one and told his secretary that it was just a lucky guess. Still, as he related the story to me, I could tell that he was torn between the reality of Inner Vision and the theory of a lucky guess. I simply told him that this was common to all my students, and I had heard countless other stories and seen many similar results. I then went on to explain that his first release had been weak only because that was the first location of the missing keys. The second, and stronger, release came because it was the exact location.

He still could not understand how his Inner Vision could have known the exact location of the keys. After all, it was not he who had put them there. I then told him that there could be three possible answers for this. First, the keys themselves are part of the spirit-that-moves-in-all-things and its force could have spoken to Greg. Second, the cleaning man also has a spiritual counterpart. Greg could have tapped into either the keys themselves or the consciousness of the cleaning man. Third, he could have simply tapped into the past history of the spirit world. I told him, however, that no matter how he located them, the results were still the same. Many times this will occur, in that we may not know where the information has come from, but we know the results to be both astounding and accurate.

A good way to illustrate how the Inner Vision speaks to us through waking visions is to use another one of my students as an example. A young girl, Sandra, was attending one of my Philosophy Workshops. She was born and raised in California, and except for attending a late November Standard Class and this Philosophy Workshop in January, she had never been to New Jersey before. In fact, up until her standard class she had not even been out of California. I only state that because the story that follows will illustrate how her Inner Vision spoke to her, conveying the very voice of the Earth. So, too, was there no way that she could have known about the plant that she was to encounter since that plant only grows in the East. Another point is that except for training at my school, she had received no other nature training, and plants in fact were her weak subject. I know that the plant she encountered is not even one of those taught at my Standard Class.

Sandy had been walking along the footpath that skirts the old and overgrown horse pasture at my farm. She felt a draw from deep inside to enter the pasture and sit down in a very specific location, which was not her original intention. She had no idea why she was drawn so strongly to the pasture and this location but she knew that she had to sit there. As she sat and gazed off in the distance and otherwise searched the field, her eyes were drawn time and time again to the stubble of a plant. All that was left of the plant was the lower part of the stem, emerging from the frozen soil barely an inch. The rest of the plant had been ravaged by the winter and had long since disappeared. She found herself gazing at the stem for longer and longer periods of time, until at one point she could look at nothing else.

Half awake and half in some ill-defined daydream, she could clearly see the entire plant and even the flower heads. She then imagined the plant boiling in water with thick clouds of steam rising. Out of nowhere came a huge eye that looked red, swollen, and very painful. As the eye passed through the steam it emerged from the other side looking healthy and without the terrible redness. She was a little shocked at all of this when she was shaken back to full consciousness by another passing student. She wandered back to the barn and laughed when she told me the story. She thought that it was all in her imagination. She so adequately described the plant to me that I gave her an identification guide and told her to look it up. To her amazement she found the plant without any trouble, even more to her amazement when she read the text and found that the plant only grew east of the Mississippi.

I then handed her one of my old and voluminous medicinal wild plant guides and again told her to look up the plant. Here she found that the Native American people used the plant for many eye infections and ailments. They would take the plant and put it into simmering water and then filter out the plant parts. They would allow the liquid to cool slightly, then use it to dampen a cloth which in turn was pressed against the closed eye. This compress was used for many infections. They would also use the cooled liquid as an eyewash. She was baffled by all of this not only because she had never seen the plant before, but because she had no idea why it had come to her in the first place. That is when I reminded her that her mother, who was also attending the class, had a sty in her eye.

It is important to note here that although this happens to my students all the time, and this is but a few examples of the countless thousands of examples I could have given, Inner Vision *must* be purified. What happened to me when I was very young, and what seems to happen to my students, is that after several dramatic successes with Inner Vision, the physical mind learns how to almost duplicate the feeling of Inner Vision and the subsequent release. It is then that the effectiveness of Inner Vision falls off. It seems to me that the logical mind is willfully trying to short-circuit the process, so that eventually we give up on Inner Vision altogether. In other words, if Inner Vision becomes inaccurate and ineffective, we will give up trying in disgust.

This is why I strongly suggest that you purify your Inner Vision. That purification method is a process you achieve only with diligent effort. Even up until a decade ago I would not completely trust my Inner Vision with the same faith Grandfather would. Though it rarely ever failed me, there were times when the results were questionable. That was mostly my fault in that I either rushed the process or I somehow allowed my physical mind to get in and pollute the results. Considering that I only began to trust my Inner Vision a decade ago, that means it took me over twenty years of diligent work to reach that point. What I tell my students is that until you have purified your Inner Vision perfectly, assume a 1 percent failure. That 1 percent is not bad, considering what you can accomplish with the other 99 percent miracles.

I also warn my students strongly that sometimes with the use of Inner Vision, you are actually staking your life on its accuracy. With a 1 percent failure margin, that is something I have only begun to do recently. For instance, Inner Vision not only reaches to the worlds beyond flesh, but also deep into your primal self. The place of instinct. Grandfather would tell me that I did not need a plant identification guide to know what plants were edible and which were medicinal. He said that the Inner Vision would provide a direct link to my instinct. The Creator gave instinct to every living creature, including man. He said, "If a young deer loses its mother right after being weaned, does he not know which plants he can eat and which he cannot? Of course he does, and so, too, with all animals. Is not man also a creature of nature?"

Simply what Grandfather was saying is that mankind has instinct for survival as does the rest of creation. Grandfather believed, and rightly so, that as man moved away from the Earth and deeper into his flesh, he began to lose that instinct. Modern man has seemed to have lost it altogether, but I am not convinced of this. So many times I have given a student a part of a plant that I knew they would not know. Locked deep in the Sacred Silence and using their Inner Vision as a guide, they have been able not only to tell me if the plant is edible or medicinal, but if it is medicinal, exactly the effect it would have on their body. Under my experimental conditions I have never seen a student fail at this. The way that this is accomplished is very simple, yet it can be very dangerous, as I will explain.

I have the student sit quietly and move deeply into the Sacred Silence. Then I place into his hand a small section of root from a South American plant. I know in my heart that he could not possibly know what plant it is, not only because it is from South America, but also because it is very rare and obscure. In fact, there are only a handful of medicine people who know what it is used for. The student then asks his Inner Vision if this plant is edible. The Inner Vision does not release, indicating that it is not edible. The student then asks if the plant is medicinal, and his Inner Vision instantly and dramatically releases, indicating that the plant has medicinal properties. The student then asks his Inner Vision where the plant will affect the body, and suddenly the Inner Vision expands to include an area of the throat. To the surprise of many the plant I chose is medicinal and is used to treat thyroid conditions. The student was right.

This is the way our ancestors used the edible, medicinal, and poisonous plants, but the process and instinct have been all but lost to modern man. Identifying plants is one of the most difficult tasks that is achieved by the Inner Vision. It is so difficult because it can be deadly. That 1 percent failure rate is still enough to kill you, and I severely recommend against all use of Inner Vision in this way. Only in the last decade have I trusted it enough to use it in this way, yet I still use a plant identification guide to prove my results. YOU MUST DO THE SAME. Grandfather was good enough to use it all the time with the edible wild plants, but that was Grandfather. I tell people not to take the chance unless you have no other choice. Finding a buried arrowhead or a lost set of keys will not kill you if you fail 1 percent of the time. Identifying wild edible and medicinal plants can.

As I said, it took me over twenty years of diligent effort to purify my Inner Vision to a point where I accept it unconditionally. You must now work to achieve that purity. The purification of Inner Vision is quite easily accomplished through the Sacred Silence. Whenever you need to ask Inner Vision, or receive a communication, it is best to go first to the deepest levels of the Sacred Silence. The Sacred Silence quiets the physical mind and allows the spiritual mind to come through. And it is through the spiritual mind where the voice of Inner Vision comes. This point of purification begins to be achieved when one goes through the meditation set forth in this book, at a place just beyond the "breath to heart" trigger. It is at this point that we begin to get a purification, where the physical mind is quieted. The more you take it to this place of purity, the purer it becomes.

Yes, it took me over twenty years of practice to reach the place of absolute purity and faith in my Inner Vision. Yet still today, under times of severe stress, it fails me, but I am aware of this place of danger and avoid it altogether. I am a hard learner, however, and I know that many can reach this point of purity faster than I could. After all, I spent much of my life learning the basic techniques I set forth in this book, techniques that you will learn in just a few days and with just a little practice. You will find that your Inner Vision not only reaches to the spirit of nature and worlds of spirit, but also to your deepest memory, your primal self, and even to your deepest instinct. Almost immediately you will find that you have a 90 percent success rate and with the Sacred Silence and some practice you will move to 99 percent success. But it will take many years and diligent effort to reach perfection.

12

The Power of
Envisioning

We now have looked at the Sacred Silence, not as an end result, as with most meditations, but as a vehicle or bridge to the worlds of the spirit of nature and the realm of spirit. However, just getting there is not enough, at least not where Grandfather was concerned. We have also learned of how we can listen to these worlds and understand what they are trying to convey to us. In this way we begin to comprehend the vast domains that have lain so far outside of our reach and are now accessible. We are now beginning to work in these outer worlds. We must understand how we can communicate with these worlds. It is not enough to get there or just to understand the voices, but we must be able to communicate our needs. Thus the circle will be complete and we can fully function there. We can now touch the "oneness," the ultimate expansion of what life is all about.

As Grandfather has said so many times: Our mind is our greatest enemy and our greatest ally. It is the part of the mind that is our ally that we use as the way of communicating our needs, desires, and spiritual directions to the vast domain of the spirit world. In order for us to communicate to the worlds beyond flesh, we must use the same language as these worlds use to reach to us. We too must learn to use the language of vision, dream, sign, symbol, and feeling. However, it is very difficult to dream exactly what we want to convey as well as being equally difficult for us to convey with signs and symbols. These things at best are far too complex for us to use with any degree of precision. That leaves waking visions and feelings as our only real means of communication.

When we look at the way our mind conjures visions, we soon observe that daydreaming, pretending, and imagining are not powerful enough. Though these things are rather free-flowing and very vivid, they lack true control, direction, and, ultimately, power. They are born more of fantasy, and in extreme cases hallucination, rather than of true spiritual reality. This leaves but one course of vision, that which most people call visualization. However, I believe, as Grandfather believed, that visualization is not enough, and this, too, lacks power. Though visualization comes closest to what is spiritually desired and has some power, it is still only two-dimensional. The visualizer is not really there. He may see the images that he wants, and even hear the images that he wants, but it is much like sitting in a theater and watching a movie. You are there, but not really part of the movie.

What then is left is what Grandfather called Envisioning. Envisioning is three-dimensional, in that you are part of what you are imagining. The best way to describe the difference between visualization and Envisioning is the way I teach the difference to my students. As you sit there reading this paragraph, close your eyes and visualize yourself being somewhere else. The feeling and imagery you get is visualization. But Envisioning is actually being someplace else and seeing yourself from that place as here, holding the book. Envisioning puts you totally here, and being someplace else is only a fleeting feeling. Envisioning is very real, and it is this authenticity and reality that gives it the ultimate power.

The Sacred Silence, meditation, and the communication of Inner Vision are certainly universal truths, common threads, which run through all religions and philosophies. So, too, is Envisioning. However, modern man has lost his power of Envisioning, and now all that is used is a crude and undirected form of Envisioning. As man grew closer to the flesh, he moved away from that which I define as Envisioning. Thus the Envisioning has lost its power. Prayer in essence is a verbal form of visualization, but I believe that mere words are not enough in true prayer. Prayer must be more Envisioned than words are in order to reach the worlds beyond the flesh. In my experience and in the experience of countless students, it is far more powerful to convey our needs through Envisioning than through prayer. The results are more dynamic and powerful.

I really believe that when we hear about the ancients speaking of prayer, they actually meant Envisioning. To them the words were but a starting point that would produce the Envisioning. They could not feel the words or become the words, but they could certainly Envision themselves feeling in their hearts what the prayers were trying to say. Envisioning put them in the reality of what they desired. They in essence became the prayer. Words are no longer important because they now live what they Envision. However, Envisioning, like prayer, still lacks the power to send the voice to the worlds beyond the flesh, unless it is accompanied by absolute belief, Inner Vision Direction, and a purpose beyond the self. I will discuss this further in the chapter on Empowering Vision, for these in themselves are as important as Envisioning. What I want to do here is to teach the reader the power of Envisioning.

The Basic Envisioning Exercise

At this point there is no need to have your partner direct the basic Envisioning exercise, for it can easily be done alone. I still stress the importance of your partner, however, for in the final analysis they will become part of your proof and bolster your belief system. It is important to also have your partner do this exercise, either with you or at some other time. It is also equally important that you do not discuss what you have seen, felt, or Envisioned during this exercise. At a later date you will share what you have done, but for right now you must keep the details to yourself.

At first this may seem like a form of self-hypnosis, but this goes far beyond any hypnosis. In the final analysis you will prove to yourself and your partner that this is not imagined but spiritually real. Very real. Yet, it is important at this point that you do not get too caught up in the question of whether this is real or imagined. For argument's sake, let us just say that what you are doing is imagined. That way you do not try so hard, it becomes free-flowing and a lot of fun. If you try too hard, then the results will be very poor. So, too, you must realize that you are in absolute control. If you do not like something that seems to pop into your Envisioning, then change it to something else. Do not say you can't. If it's there and you imagined it, then you have the power to take it away.

In this basic Envisioning exercise there are three worlds: the path, the stairs, and what I call the Medicine Place. I recommend that you keep all of these areas as natural as possible, without the influence of any man-made things. After all, man-made things are of the flesh and not a reality in the world of nature and certainly not needed in the world of spirit. However, if these man-made things make you feel more comfortable in your imagined surroundings, then by all means keep them there. I just find that my students, as a whole, do far better without the distractions of any symbols of the flesh. Now, keeping this in mind, I would like to deal with each of the three imagined places individually.

Now imagine a path, or trail, that you can walk down. The trail can be any trail that makes you feel good. The trail I used when I was a child was a deep forest trail, leading through my beloved Pine Barrens. Yours can be a trail through mountains, deserts, jungles, grasslands, or anything that you like. You may even use a trail that exists in flesh reality and add things to that existing trail. I find that my students get the best results using their favorite trail and adding more imagined things to its overall personality.

The steps are usually made of old stone and lead down off the trail to the right, terminating at an archway or some sort of doorway. Again, you can create any kind of stairs that you like and any kind of doorway that you like. Most of my students prefer the stone steps and an archway made also of stone. It is on the other side of the archway that exists the world of your Medicine Place.

Your Medicine Place is a very special place. It is a place of many dimensions, landscapes, and feelings. In it you can create anything you want, any kind of landscape or combinations of landscapes. It can consist of a landscape you know to exist in reality and can be surrounded by many imagined landscapes. In this place you are like a god. You can fly, swim underwater for hours, create things at will, walk with the animals, fly with the birds, speak to the fish, anything you want. Most of all it is a place where you are strong, relaxed and peaceful, secure, healthy, and happy. It is a place to play, forget the fretting, striving, and slaving of the outside world of flesh, and become a child again. It is a place of ultimate freedom.

It is important that you make all of these places—the trail, the stairs, and the Medicine Place—as real as possible. You want to use all of your senses in wandering through these places. The purer the Envisioning, the more real they become. In fact, to my students these places become so real, so much fun, that they do not want to return to flesh reality. All come back from their Medicine Places refreshed, relaxed, and strong. It is truly a delight and a reprieve from everyday life. Again, it is not important to wonder whether these places are real or imagined; just keep them imagined for right now—though after you visit them, you will think otherwise. Now let's begin our journey through these imagined worlds.

I suggest strongly that you begin this exercise lying down in a comfortable position. Get to a place, like your bedroom, where you will not be disturbed. Remember that there is a fine line at first between sleep and meditation, so you want to focus fully on what you are doing. If you lose your concentration, you may fall asleep. If you live in a noisy environment, you may want to put on some soft New Age–type music in the background to muffle any outside distracting sounds.

I began doing this exercise with Grandfather lying on a mossy bank beside a quiet little stream and used the sounds of nature for my background music. In an indoor environment you can also use a tape of natural sounds with the same results. In this exercise I will use the places that I once used as a child to help direct your Envisioning process. Remember, however, that you can change any of these things, for my places are but used as a starting reference point.

To begin your Envisioning exercise, you should go through the entire Sacred Silence exercise, ending with several "breath to heart" sequences to make sure you are firmly there. Now Envision yourself standing at the beginning of your trail. Before you begin to walk, make sure that you see the trail through your own imagined eyes, feel the earth beneath your feet, smell the freshness of the air, hear the wind in the trees, the calling of the birds, and the symphony of nature. Feel yourself being there totally, using all of your senses of sight, sound, taste, smell, touch, and sense of gravity and position. Now begin your walk slowly. With each step use all of your senses, feel the motion of your body, and see through your own imagined eyes. Again, the more you can become the picture, and the more you see through your imagined eyes and sense through the imagined senses, the more vivid and real it becomes.

As you continue along your trail, with each step, feel a deep relaxation and peace sweep over you. Your journey should last several minutes, but time is something that is nonexistent in the Sacred Silence. As you near the end of the trail, you will note a set of stairs leading down and to your right. They are old stone steps, as if carved from the very bedrock of the earth. Approach the top of the stairs and look down to an archway at the bottom. Pouring through the archway is a brilliant sunlight. You can sense the purity of the light, its peace, and healing qualities. Now begin to walk down the stairs, feeling yourself relaxing and concentrating even more than when you were on your forest path. Again, see the stairs through your own imagined eyes, rather than watching yourself walking. Use all of your senses, making it as vivid and real as possible. I tell my students to make but ten steps so that this process goes by easily.

As you approach closer to the light, feel it first hitting your feet and warming them. Feel the healing properties of the light that pours through your archway, and with each step taken feel the light hitting farther and farther up your body. Finally you are standing at the last step, feeling the warmth of the light bathing your entire body. You look at your archway, imagining that it is the gateway to your own private world. A world where you know nothing but joy, peace, health, and security. A world without limitations or problems. A place where all things live in balance and harmony, where you are a god, capable of doing anything and everything. Most of all it is a world where you have complete control over all things, where you can create miracles. You can feel the power of your Medicine Place even before you pass through the archway.

Now pass through your archway and cast your eyes on the breathtaking beauty of your world. You may see mountains and lush valleys, jungles and beautiful beaches, waterfalls, animals, caves, birds, fish and dolphins, wild flowers, quiet pools of water, and hot springs. You create all the trees, flowers, and landscapes to your liking. Use places that make you feel so good, so at peace, and so powerful. Some of you will add places that you know to exist in the reality of flesh. One landscape of jungle can border on another of a desert. It makes no difference in this place, for you can have anything you want and banish the things that you don't want. After all, it is your world and in it you are a god. If you feel that you

cannot change something you don't like, then it is only the
limitations of your own mind. Eventually, however, through
repeated visits, the landscapes will remain unchanged. This
is only how it should be.

While in your Medicine Place, swim with the dolphins,
fly with the birds, travel through the mystery of caves and
caverns, pet the animals, smell the flowers, climb the trees
and mountains, stand beneath the waterfalls. Anything you
want you can do, but most of all have fun and become
a carefree child again. Giggle and laugh, roll in the mud,
body-surf the waves, dance freely and joyfully, and feel
the peace and power sweep over you. Sense the magnifi-
cence and grandeur. Know that anything and everything is
possible. Feel the healing of body, mind, and spirit and
know that you are whole. Pour your senses into this place,
see it through your imagined eyes, feel the sensations of
everything that you do. It is important here to note that
you do not want the influence of any imagined people in
your Medicine Place at first. Later you can add anything
you want. Just for now, keep with the natural theme free of
mankind, other than yourself. It's also fine and fun to take
on the shape of an animal if you wish and change that shape
as you wish.

Now when you want to return to the reality of the physical
world, begin to work your way back to the archway. Pass
through the archway and begin to climb the imaginary stairs,
feeling your strength returning with each step taken. When
you reach the last step, shift your consciousness back into
your physical body. Slowly begin to stretch, moving your
arms and legs slightly. Then slowly and carefully come to
a full sitting position, waiting for a few moments before
you stand. You will note that I made your imagined journey
almost a complete circle, where you end by coming back up
the imagined stairs. I find that it is best to do all things in
this manner, for it gives far better results. So in everything
you do, try to keep it cyclical. Whenever my students are
having problems, it is usually because they did not keep
their meditations cyclical.

That reminds me of a story that Grandfather once told me dealing with this cyclic approach. A young man sat Envisioning himself picking up a large stone. Each time he started Envisioning, he would physically get up and try to lift the stone. Time after time he failed. Seeing this, his elder came to him and asked him what he was doing. The young man told the elder what he was attempting to do. The elder asked the young man what he was Envisioning. He told him that he Envisioned himself bending down and lifting the stone easily. The elder smiled at him and said that it was but half the story. He also needed to put the stone back down. With his next Envisioning the young man saw himself lifting the stone and putting it back down. He then was able to physically lift the stone.

It is important that you should not tell your partner any detail of your imagined walk along the trail, your stairs, and especially your Medicine Place. I strongly suggest to my students that they make several imagined journeys into their Medicine Place, each time making it more vivid and real until it becomes very familiar. It is also best during the first several imagined journeys that you lie down in a quiet environment so that there are few distractions. Right now it is important to make your imagined Medicine Place as real and familiar as possible.

The Journey

With the repeated journeys to your Medicine Place, many of you are beginning to wonder whether this place is real or imagined. Simply, it is real. This place has always been there, and I feel that it is our personal place in the spiritual world. It is definitely our birthright to go to this place and a gift to us all from the Creator. I believe and I know that each person has his or her own Medicine Place, unique from all the rest. In fact, it is at this point when you can no longer change the landscapes in your Medicine Place that you have finally arrived at its reality. You may attempt to change the place, but it will always come back to what it was. That's fine, for that is how it is supposed to be. Now you may ask: How do I know that it is real? My answer is, because you can take someone there. You cannot take someone to an imagined place.

You and your partner should go to a quiet room where you can lie or sit side by side without distractions. It might be a good idea to use a background music, natural sound, and conditions that you are both familiar with; that way the newness of the situation will not become a distraction to your partner. You both should decide on a signal to use when the journey will begin. I suggest that a simple squeeze of the hand or a tug on the arm will be enough of a signal so that your partner will know when to begin. Finally you must then decide who is going to be the host and who will be the visitor. It is important when the journey begins that the host be a strong leader, showing the visitor the important features of his Medicine Place. The visitor should remain as open and free of outside thought as possible, taking note of anything he or she sees along the way.

Once all variables have been taken care of, it is time to begin the journey. Lying, reclining, or sitting side by side, the host should either hold the visitor's hand or grasp the sleeve. This physical attachment seems to lend reinforcement to the Envisioning process and tends to maintain the roles of host and visitor. The process should begin with both of you going through your Sacred Silence meditation so that you are both equally relaxed and the mind is focused. As soon as the host reaches the end of the "breath to heart" sequence, he should imagine himself standing at the beginning of his trail holding the arm or hand of the visitor. Now with a slight physical and Envisioned squeeze of the hand or a tug on the sleeve, the journey will begin. At this point it is fine that you Envision yourself letting go of your partner, though on a physical level remain holding his hand or sleeve.

The host should be a very strong and vivid leader. He should Envision his partner walking along the path with him, purposely showing him the various points of interest and other specific things, such as flowers, certain trees, the kind of path, and even pointing out various animals. He should continue leading his visitor along the path and to the stairs. Here he should pause for a moment and point out to his visitor the kind of stairs and show them the arch or doorway at the bottom of the stairs. The journey continues down the stairs and the host again shows the visitor the points of interest as well as specific things about the stairs and what is around them. Again, the host must be a strong leader, while the visitor remains very open.

Now the real fun begins as the host leads the visitor through the arch or doorway. Here the visitor becomes almost as powerful as the host and is able to fly, breathe underwater, pet the animals, and do many other marvelous things. The visitor should remember that he cannot change things in this landscape for he is only visiting. This should hardly be mentioned because the visitor is open and passive, rather than active in this Envisioning. Now even more than ever the host should be even stronger, showing the visitor the landscapes, taking him on journeys, but most of all keeping a sense of fun and excitement. The host should also point out very specific things and undertake very specific adventures, making sure to Envision his visitor being with him the entire time.

After a while the journey comes to an end, and both of you will again pass through the archway. At this point the host should squeeze the visitor's hand or tug lightly on his shirtsleeve to let his partner know that he has now passed through the arch or doorway. Now you can both go up the stairs and back into your physical bodies independently. Once you are both fully awake, you will probably sit in discussion for an hour or more. The visitor will tell the host everything that has come into his mind. It is important that the visitor convey to the host any sensations, feelings, and even unexplained images. For instance, if the visitor felt as if he were swimming, flying, sliding, or playing, these should all be conveyed. Colors, smells, sounds, and even images that seem to make no connection at all to the exercise should also be talked about.

Be careful, though, that you do not discount things that do not seem to make sense at first. I once had a student get a sensation of sliding down a snowy hillside, but could not correlate it with the journey to the host's Medicine Place. Upon further searching the host said that he did take her sliding down a smooth frothy white waterfall, equal to the slope of a hillside. Another time a host took his visitor for a flight on the back of an eagle, and the visitor saw flight on an eagle's feather. Another visitor saw patterns of flowers on a soft comforter as he and his partner rolled on it. His partner said that they were rolling down a soft hillside spangled lavishly with all sorts of flowers. So, too, another student got the image of a bear's nose while his partner said that he was showing him how to pet his big friendly bear.

Some of my students ask me at this point if this is not just the act of reading his partner's mind. This can be quickly discounted with the mentioning of one simple fact. More often than not the visitor will pick up images and places that are part of the host's Medicine Place that the host did not actually point out or take him to. If this were the act of simple mind reading, then the visitor could only pick up the things that the host had pointed out or Envisioned taking the visitor to. So, too, you will find that there are a few things that your visitor did not pick up on. This is probably due to the fact that you and your partner have not yet reached a point of pure mind, which will take quite some time. In any meditation all of us wrestle with stray thoughts that are not related to the Envisioning exercises.

In a typical basic Philosophy Workshop I find that nearly 85 percent of my students get solid success, with a few getting fair results, and fewer still getting nothing at all. If you are in the last category, then do not get upset and get down on yourself. You have done nothing wrong. I find that those students who initially have trouble have fantastic successes with the next attempt. It sometimes takes the initial journey to allow the visitor to let go of his fears and be open to the experience. So, too, are there many other factors that could interfere with the journey, such as not being in the right frame of mind to begin with, outside distractions, or not feeling physically well. Simply, give it time and it will work for anyone.

Once my students realize that this place does exist, they first ask where is it. I tell them that these Medicine Places are our little homes in the spirit world. It is there that we can work miracles, because the spirit world knows no limitations, time, or place. They also ask, "What can we do?" and "How can we make these miracles happen?" It is probably the same question you are asking yourself. I have them begin with a simple Envisioning which produces such astounding results that it borders on the miraculous. This shows the student just what is possible in the world of the spirit. And from this success, I can then lead them to infinite miracles.

The Sacred Place

Now, after you have visited your Medicine Place for a while and have become very familiar and secure there, I want you to find or create a special place within the Medicine Place. A place where you feel the most comfortable, secure, healthy, and most of all, powerful. It is a place that you consider to be the center of your Medicine Place. In this special place make sure that you can stand, sit, or recline easily and comfortably. You may want to mark this special place with a circle of small rocks, the same as I did when I first created my place. This way it tends to be set apart from all the rest. I considered this place to be the center of my spiritual universe. Grandfather called it our Sacred Place. I also suggest that in one part of your Sacred Place, near its edge, place a large boulder with a flat top that just comes to your waist. It should be long enough and wide enough for someone to lie down on. However, this boulder should not be placed in the center of your Sacred Place.

Simply this Sacred Place is your workroom, the place where you will work miracles in the world of spirit. This is where most of your spiritual work will begin and end. It is always a place that we come to begin a task, and obeying the cyclic laws, it is where we will end a spiritual task. It is our place of power. Nothing can harm us when we are there, because we are all powerful in this place. All things are possible from the center of this place provided they are first guided by Inner Vision and the power of faith. You should go to this place several times before you undertake this next exercise. That way your starting and finishing point will be powerful.

Spirit Journey

This next exercise is geared to give my students a taste of what is possible from their Sacred Place in the spirit world. It also creates a need to go on and learn more, a need to help create miracles. You must first choose a place close by, within walking distance of where you will do this meditation. It must be a place you have never explored before but know to exist. I do not suggest a place that you must drive to because that becomes far too complicated for the beginning journey. Keep it simple. Once this place is chosen in your mind, then it is time to prepare for the Spirit Journey exercise. Again, you must find a place free of distraction and one that is comfortable, so that you can fully concentrate on the Sacred Silence and the Envisioning that follows.

Reclining or sitting comfortably, go deep into the Sacred Silence, again ending with a "breath to heart" sequence. Then you will journey along your path, down your stairs, through the arch and into the Medicine Place. Play there for a while. You do not want to rush. You should now enter your Sacred Area and recline in as much the same way as you are in the reality of flesh. You may find that it is hard at times to separate the world of flesh from the world of spirit, but this is very normal and should not become a distraction. Now Envision that your Sacred Place is slowly changing and becoming exactly like the place you have chosen to do this exercise. Make this Envisioning as vivid and real as possible. You may be delighted to find that this is quite easy since you are already there in the flesh.

Now, without opening your eyes or moving on a physical level, Envision yourself slowly standing up and looking around. You may look back at your body reclining there, but some people find this to be frightening or distracting. In spiritual reality you have nothing to fear. Envision yourself walking toward the unexplored place you have chosen, feeling yourself making each step, seeing the landscape pass, hearing the sounds, and feeling all the sensations. Make it as real as possible. Continue your journey to this unexplored place and begin to explore it fully. Look at the pattern of the trees and brush, and the lay of the land, listen to the sounds, look at specific things and also things in general. Pay close attention to any symbols that may appear or any sensations you may feel no matter how out of place they seem.

After you have explored the area well, begin your return journey. Remember to keep it as real as possible. Continue to walk back to your Envisioned body and slowly get back. Feel your body shift slightly with the process. Now, as you lie there for a few moments, begin to change the area back into your Sacred Place. Envision yourself arising from your position and moving back toward the archway, then up the stairs and back into your physical body. This completes the cyclic process. Now it's time to go out and explore the unexplored area in physical reality. You will be amazed or even shocked at the results. There will be no doubt in your mind that you have been there, for you have seen it all in your Envisioning. This will probably leave you searching for answers as to how it happened. Simply answered: You walked there in spirit.

You will have proved to yourself that not only the spiritual world exists beyond all doubt, but you can actually work there and create miracles. But about the people that get poor results or none at all? If you got poor results or none at all, you were probably distracted, but there can be other reasons for this which I will set forth in the next chapter. Be careful, however, in deciding that you received poor results, because sometimes great results can be masked. Remember, many of you are just beginning to exercise your spiritual minds, and you may lack precision, control, and perception. These will grow stronger with time. So, too, remember that the logical mind is always quick to jump in and try to interpret before the full spiritual image makes itself manifest. Let me give you a few examples of students who thought they got poor results but actually got fantastic results when observed realistically.

One of my students took this Spirit Journey only to find a blue golf ball that glistened in the sun, as if made of some metallic substance. He could not even bring himself to leave the workshop area and see if he had been right. In his thinking, there could be no golf ball in the middle of the woods, far less one made of some metallic blue substance. Upon my urging he went out to the area he had chosen only to find that there was a tightly rolled-up ball of blue metallic gift wrap, about the size of a golf ball. It was exactly in the same location and lying in the same position he had seen in his Envisioning. I later told him it was his logical mind that had jumped in and determined the object had to be a golf ball, instead of tightly balled wrapping paper, but I also said that it was close enough.

Another one of my students saw in his Envisioning a clear image of a tight, brown, spiraling, round cave with a shiny white boulder in the bottom. He, like my first student, discounted it completely, deciding it was more of an image, or geometric symbol, rather than reality. He thought it could not possibly be found in or around the landscape he had explored in his Envisioning. I encouraged him to go out and see what he could find. I could tell on his return from the startled look on his face that he had found exactly what he had seen. He told me that he had entered the unexplored area, sat down and carefully looked around but could find nothing like the symbol that he had seen. Just as he was about to give up, he looked down at his feet and to his amazement there lay a huge rusted nut from an old carriage. In its center lay a shiny white stone. It was exactly as he had seen it only smaller. Again the logical mind had jumped in too soon and decided it to be a cave rather than the smaller carriage nut.

Another one of my students did very well with the exercise. He saw many things that were actually in the place. However, there was one thing that had come to him in the most vivid way, but he could not find it no matter how hard he looked. He could not understand why he had done so well with all the other images that had come to him, yet with the strongest one he had failed. What he had seen was a large wooded wine rack, but unlike a classic wine rack, this one had rectangular holders. As he gave up and walked back to the workshop area, he tripped over something hidden partially by underbrush. As he looked back to see what he had tripped over, he gasped in amazement. There tangled in his feet was the exact wine rack he saw in his Envisioning. But instead of a wine rack, it was an old and neatly folded section of rusted sheep fence. Until he inspected it more closely, it looked identical to the wine rack he had seen.

These are but a few examples of the people who think that they had poor results only to find that they had fantastic, miraculous results. You must remember that even though your physical/logical mind is quiet from the Sacred Silence, and the power of the Envisioning is stronger, the mind is still quick to jump in and try to define, qualify, and analyze. The physical mind will be less apt to do so as the spiritual mind gains power and control. It is only a matter of time and practice. But alas, the journey with a visitor to your Medicine Place and the Journey of the Spirit are very weak, and only give us a taste of what is possible. For the results to be stronger and purer, there must be the Power. Without it the results will only remain miraculous but weak. What we must do now is to give the Sacred Silence the Power to work miracles beyond description.

13

The Elements of Power

Grandfather said, "We are not the power, nor is it we who create the miracles. It is the power of Creation, the spirit world, and the Creator working through us. We are but a bridge for that power, as is anyone who knows the simple truth. We must never take credit for what we have helped to do, but hide the fact that we are the bridge. Self-glorification is the lust of the physical mind. To know the truth is to know that we have done nothing but be used by the forces outside of ourselves. It is then not we who create the Power, for we only obey and direct its forces. We are nothing more than a hollow vessel. We simply obey the commands. The Power is given to us to command and direct. Without the command or the Power, we are but an empty vessel."

What Grandfather was saying was clearly stated above. It is not we who create the miracles, but the worlds of nature, spirit, and the Creator working through us. He also said so many times that we must hide the fact that we have any power at all. The ego can destroy the vessel and could close the doorway forever. So, too, can the ego and lust for power lead us to seek the power of the demons from the Dark Side. That line between Good and Evil is very thin indeed. Evil does not need our belief to give it power, for it has power enough. We see it rear its ugly head throughout the world today, every day. It is the fears of man, his lust for riches, his greed, and the sins of the flesh which nourish that Evil and give it such an awesome power. This is why we can do nothing without being guided by the Light, the Goodness, of the spirit.

To work any power or miracle for self-gratification is to negate the effort. We can do nothing and can decide nothing by ourselves. We must be directed before anything can be empowered. We may desperately want to do something, but unless inwardly directed and empowered, we can do nothing. So, too, if we are directed and do become the vessel for a miracle, and glorify ourselves amongst our peers, then the Power will be taken from us, sometimes forever. So, there is nothing we can do without the direction and the Power. What follows are the elements needed before we can become empowered to do anything. Without this Power, all we attempt to do will fail or be weak at best. The elements are as follows.

Inner Vision Direction

All of our spiritual actions must be directed by the Power of Inner Vision. Just wanting to do something and wanting it badly is not enough. The voice and the command must come to us through the Power of Inner Vision. Remember that Grandfather considered Inner Vision to be the very voice of the Creator. Thus, no one is a more powerful bridge than another, for without Inner Vision there can be no bridge. You may not be called to use the Power while a peer is strongly called, and at other times you may be called while he is not. So then who is stronger? No one and everyone. So

Inner Vision Direction is the first element that empowers the envisioning and creates what is desired and needed.

Faith

Grandfather said that faith is the most powerful force on Earth and in the world of spirit. It is not just the faith in the spirit realms and faith in the Creator, but faith that can move mountains, heal the sick, create miracles, and otherwise do what physical man considers impossible. Without this unwavering faith there can be no bridge, no Power, and no miracles. We are fortunate that at first our faith can be weak, yet we can create miracles, and as we mature spiritually, so, too, does our faith mature in the powers beyond that of physical man. It is this unwavering faith that transcends all limitation.

The Sacred Silence and Envisioning

These two elements must be in the purest and strongest form in order for us to succeed as a bridge for the Power. The Sacred Silence must be so powerful that all outside distractions are transcended and we are firmly placed into the realm of spirit. It is the Sacred Silence that gives us pure mind. The spiritual mind enables us to communicate with the world of spirit and the spirit world to clearly communicate with us. So, too, must our Envisioning be so pure and powerful that we are actually part of what we Envision. We are so thoroughly caught up in what is being Envisioned that there is no world outside of that Envisioned world. But even if the Power of the Sacred Silence and Envisioning is strong indeed, we can do nothing without Inner Vision Direction and Faith.

Purpose Beyond Self

I believe that if you are directed by Inner Vision to do something, then the purpose will always be beyond self. Yet I do believe that this also must be defined again in the elements needed for the Power. In whatever we do spiritually, even in practice, we cannot do it for ourselves or self-glorification. We must transcend the self in all ways. If we practice our spiritual skill only for ourselves, then it will not work. But if we practice with the sole purpose of helping others, then it is beyond self and the purpose is pure. Only when we reach out beyond self and work selflessly can we ever hope to become a pure and powerful bridge.

These elements of Inner Vision Direction—Faith, pure and powerful Sacred Silence and Envisioning, and the Purpose Beyond Self—are the elements that make up the Power. In order for us to accomplish anything spiritually at all these elements must be satisfied. If but one is weak, then we will fail, or receive poor results. Thus, before attempting anything spiritually, we must make sure that all of these elements are in place. However, I believe that the two most powerful of these elements are Faith and Inner Vision Direction. The rest can be weak, and yet we can still perform miracles of lasting value. This is a tremendous asset to us, for as we begin on our spiritual path, our Envisioning and Sacred Silence may be weak, but we can still be used as a bridge.

A very powerful example of these elements can be illustrated in the following story of Grandfather and an old woman. We were relaxing at Grandfather's camp one evening when the stillness was shattered by a rather distraught voice calling Grandfather's name. At first I thought it was from the spirit world, but with the subsequent brush-ruffling and footfalls I knew that the caller was of flesh. Grandfather sent us to fetch the person and lead him back to camp. I could tell Grandfather knew exactly who he was and why he was coming, even before we heard his call the first time. Grandfather had an uncanny ability to know of things long before they occurred, for he lived the duality constantly and religiously. He was always connected to things outside the realm of the scenes, always listening to the distant voice, and always fused to the greater consciousness. He seemed to be a direct link to the "force," the spirit-that-moves-in-all-things, and "one" with all things, flesh and spirit.

We slipped through the swamp, down the deer trail, and to the old sand road, following the voice to its origin. We found an older gentleman who had been wandering back and forth along the trail calling Grandfather's name and trying to locate his camp. Neither Rick nor I had ever seen him before. He was wearing clothing and shoes that told us he was from a town and not living in the woods like the people of the Pines. I led him back to camp and introduced him to Grandfather. Grandfather seemed to know who he was and why he was there. As Grandfather spoke, the man was visibly amazed at how much Grandfather knew of his situation and plight.

The man's mother was dying and in a coma. She had been to doctors for many years and had spent considerable time on medication for cancer. The cancer now infected her entire body, and she was close to death. Apparently she had been hospitalized for quite some time and fell into the coma there. Her last request was that she die at home, and she was subsequently moved there the day before. The doctors said she had only a few hours to live and was failing fast. The priest had already given her the last rites, and the family was waiting for her at bedside to die. Apparently the man had heard of Grandfather from an old Piney chicken farmer and now had come to find him. Though the family did not believe in herbal medicine or the old ways, Grandfather was the last resort, and the man was willing to try anything to save his mother. His voice and actions seemed desperate, and he still contained a paradoxical disbelief in Grandfather's ability to do anything. Before we left, the man asked Grandfather not to tell the family that he was an herbalist or to show any mystical abilities. This would only upset the family.

He left camp and traveled home. We were brought to the house, and the man told his family that Grandfather was an old friend of his mother's and wanted to see her alone. With reluctance the family left the room, but the man stayed, refusing to leave. Grandfather turned to me and whispered, "Get me a glass of water for the old woman." But what about the herbs, I asked? Grandfather said hoarsely, "Do as you are told." I went to the kitchen to get a glass of water. I could not see what good water was going to do, or how he was going to get her to drink it, as she was in a deep coma. I returned quickly and handed Grandfather the water. He winked at me and with a half smile whispered, "This is for the man's benefit, not his mother's." With that, Grandfather slowly slipped his hands under the old woman's neck and lifted her forward. Her body was frail, skin covering bones and not much else. Her lifeless gray color foretold of the closeness of death. With the other hand, he placed his fingers in the water and transferred a drop to her lips. With that, he laid her back down, placing one hand on her head, the other on her stomach. The man sat by, mute and motionless, with a solemn, agonizing expression on his face.

The room was lit only with a small lamp in the corner, casting the bed into deep shadows of grayness. I watched Grandfather slowly bow his head in prayer, his hands still firmly planted on her lifeless body. Suddenly I saw Grandfather's body start to vibrate slightly, almost imperceptibly. In the dim room I could see his hands, as if they glowed, and I had to shake my head to make sure I wasn't seeing things. At that moment, like a dull flash, the old woman's body glowed, also, as if illuminated from within, then her body fell back into the original shadow. Grandfather slowly removed his hands, and the old woman groaned. Her skin now looked white, not the dull, transparent gray it had been before. The old woman began to stir a bit; obviously she was coming out of the coma. The man jumped to his feet, staring in utter disbelief.

Grandfather looked at him and said, "I go now. Do not tell anyone what you have witnessed here." The man began to speak, but Grandfather cut him short, saying, "Do not be amazed at what you have seen here, for the ancient herbs are sometimes more powerful than your modern ways." The man began to thank Grandfather profusely, but again Grandfather cut him short. "There is no need to thank me," he said, "for I have done nothing. I am just a bridge for the force of Creation." With that, the man fell silent, and Grandfather said confidently, "She will walk within the hour but have no recollection of what has taken place. She will be restored to full health within seven suns." Without another word, Grandfather left the house. The man stared at me and I at him, both of us in utter disbelief. As I left the house, I heard the old woman call her son's name, and the family rushed by me. I cried like a baby, for I was certain that I had witnessed a full miracle.

I followed Grandfather back to camp. Not a word was exchanged. My mind was filled with more questions than I had ever had. How could a glass of water make a person well, what was the strange glow I had seen in Grandfather's hand, and what kind of medicine did he use? These were just a few of the most pressing questions. I had heard of faith healing, but I knew faith healing had more to do with a person's faith than with the healer. In essence, a faith healer is nothing more than a catalyst for the patient to focus upon. The patient is so convinced of the faith healer's power that it sets the patient into self-imposed recovery. It is the patient who heals himself, through faith. Grandfather had healed someone who was in a coma and for a family that did not believe in things of the unseen and eternal. How could he have possibly accomplished this healing, for there were no herbs and no faith? My mind overflowed, and I was overwhelmed with the rapture of it all. I had borne witness to the impossible.

I sat at camp, staring into the fire in silence. I watched Grandfather moving about camp as if nothing out of the ordinary had happened this night. I held him in awe; my heart felt like I was in the presence of a deity. He glanced toward me and searched me with his eyes, and I could feel them reading my soul. He said, "Do not hold me above all else, for I have done nothing. I am but a bridge for the force of Creation to flow from, and I do nothing that any man, who knows the truth, cannot do." He continued, "The water was not the healer. The water was a crutch for the man to feed upon while I directed the spirit-that-moves-in-all-things to heal the woman. The water was merely a camouflage for those who witnessed but did not believe. It was not my power that healed the old woman, but the Power of Creation's life force surging through me. You, too, must learn that all the tools and remedies of man are but mere camouflages, crutches for those who do not believe. You must learn to control and use this life force, for that is the only healing."

As you can clearly see, with this healing all the elements were in place and in fact very pure and powerful. Grandfather knew that the man would be coming even before he appeared on the trail. Thus, his Inner Vision had already communicated with him. The Power of Grandfather's Sacred Silence and Envisioning transcended anything I could ever hope to achieve today. His purpose was well beyond self, for he denied what he had done and actually went to the trouble of moving the camp so that no one could find him. Finally his belief was so powerful that there was no doubt in his mind that this old woman would walk again. As a child I could not even conceive in my wildest imagination of such a powerful faith. Even now as I think of it, there is a sense of awe that brings tears to my eyes, such was the power of his conviction and belief.

Another example of the use of the elements of Power was found in the story of Misha. Misha was in one of my first philosophy classes and very eager to learn all that he could of Grandfather's spiritual ways. He had searched his whole life for spiritual enlightenment but had found no real path that satisfied him. All he found was a world of complication, embellished with all manner of religious toys and impossible doctrines. Finally, when he got to my school, he said that deep inside he knew that this might be the answer to what he had searched for. He seemed to excel in all the basic exercises, surpassing much of the class in his abilities. That is, until it came to the Journeys of the Spirit. Here he failed miserably, or so he thought.

During the Spirit Journey exercise he could not imagine the unexplored landscape and had nothing to contribute to the class other than saying that he must not be worthy of this particular skill. He tried several more times for the rest of the week but still could not get any results. The more he tried to Envision himself walking away to explore, the more he seemed to be locked into his body. When he left at the end of the class, he was very happy with all that he had accomplished, but he told me that he was upset that he had done so poorly on the spirit-walking exercises. I just told him that the time was probably not right for him yet, but it would come eventually, especially when needed.

Nearly six months later he returned to take the Advanced Philosophy Workshop. When I did get time to talk to him, he told me that he had done well with his meditations but that he still could not go on a Spiritual Journey with any success. At best all that he was able to accomplish was to briefly leave his body, that which modern man calls "out-of-body experience," but he felt that it lacked any real purpose. That was all to change during an evening break midweek through the class. It was then that Misha had a profound success.

Misha had done well with the advanced spiritual studies all week, but still he could do nothing with the Journey of the Spirit. Just after dinner one night he decided to go out to the old oak tree on my farm and meditate for a while to clear his mind. He easily slipped into the Sacred Silence, but then, for some reason, he felt himself flying high above himself. His Inner Vision beckoned him to go home in a very powerful way. Without hesitation he Envisioned himself flying over the landscape, changing the landscapes, as he headed toward his home in California. He Envisioned himself then hovering high above his house. So powerful indeed was this Envisioning that he lost all consciousness of being physically back at the old oak tree.

He Envisioned himself passing through the roof of his home, down through the upper bedroom and into the living room. To his shock and horror, there lay his elderly mother on the living room floor, clutching her chest in an apparent unconscious agony. Suddenly there was a surge of energy, and he found himself back in his body at the old oak tree. Without hesitation he began to rush back to the farm, worried that his Envisioning might be correct, such was the anxiety in his heart. His run slowed to a walk, however, as he approached the barn. He began to doubt what he had witnessed and decided not to mention it at all. As the hours passed by his anxiety became so overwhelming that he approached me with his story, hoping that I would be of some help.

He told me of what he had seen and how real it had all been. He also told me that the feeling of anxiety would not leave him and that was why he was coming to me for help. He said that the Envisioning did not make any sense. He lived in his house alone, and his elderly mother lived several blocks away with his sister. There was no way that she could be in the house, especially without his sister there. I told him not to hesitate and to call his sister's house. He ran to the phone and called, and I could see the immediate relief wash over him when his sister answered. However, this was replaced by the look of utter horror when his sister told him that she had dropped their mother off at his house hours before, to quietly relax while her house was being painted. He demanded that his sister get right over to his house without delay, not giving any details as to why.

He tried calling his house several times over the next hour, but there was no answer. There was no answer from his sister's house either, and he began to think the worse possible scenario. I told him that his mother would be fine, for that is why he had been directed to take the Spirit Journey to his house in the first place. After more than an hour his sister called my school, and Misha was relieved to learn that his mother was resting comfortably in the hospital. She had suffered a mild heart attack and had gone unconscious at his home. His sister had gotten to his house and called the ambulance just in time. She was curious, however, as to how he had known that there was something wrong. Misha just told her that he had a feeling that their mother might need help. Subsequently his sister did not buy into his explanation and ended up coming to the next class.

Misha was amazed and told me so as he packed up to go home so he could be with his mother. He could not understand why the Spirit Journey had worked so well this time, especially after all of the failures. I told him that he had been called by Inner Vision and with a very powerful purpose. The Sacred Silence and Envisioning were thus empowered by the calling, and there had been no room for disbelief. He had been empowered by all of the elements of Power and was able to take the miraculous Spirit Journey which saved his mother's life. We may want to do something spiritually in the worst way, but unless we satisfy the elements of power, we can do nothing.

14

Journey of the Shaman

In Grandfather's mind a shaman was one who transcended the very religion that brought him to the final path of enlightenment. The shaman needed no religious toys or crutches, no ceremony, custom, gaudy religious dogmas, no cathedrals, or any sacred artifacts. The shaman needed nothing but the purity of his own spiritual mind. Grandfather believed that there was no right or wrong religion or belief, for they all led up the mountain of spiritual enlightenment. However, at one point, far up the mountain, all of these paths came together and fused into one well-defined trail. That is the path of the shaman, where all come together as one, where all speak a common tongue, and religious beliefs and differences are cast aside. It is this path that we should all seek. A path of purity, without the need for man's complications and gaudy religious doctrines.

This was Grandfather's quest, to find the simple and pure path, free from the distractions of man's religions. He felt that if people could find this simple freedom, then they could immediately walk this shamanic pathway. So much time was wasted in learning particular doctrines, only to ultimately be abandoned once man reached spiritual enlightenment. That time, those countless years, could be used for better things, rather than to stagnate in some cathedral reading of others' miracles. So what then is the role of the shaman? What is his ultimate Quest? Grandfather felt that it was to become 'a bridge for the power of creation and for the Creator. A bridge that healed the Earth and all the things of the Earth, making life truly rich, free from the sins of the flesh. It is to leave our children a legacy of love and purity, rather than a world of hatred and greed.

So it is the quest of the shaman to heal. Heal on a physical, emotional, mental, and spiritual level, all things of the Earth and sky. We are part of a whole, a collective consciousness that encompasses all things. If one part of the whole is sick and hurting, then all is sick. We ourselves are sick and cannot be whole until all is whole. Healing can be a gentle touch or caress to a friend in need; it can be as simple as picking up a piece of paper, teaching children to respect the Earth and Creator, or as profound as the healing Grandfather helped bring about in that old woman riddled with cancer. Healing takes on many forms and has many purposes, but the grand purpose is to make things whole, living in balance and harmony with creation, each other, and the Creator. So the power in the shamanic path is the healing, and it is what this chapter will focus upon.

What follows are the four basic skills of the shaman. I qualify them all under the category of healing. Whether it is a communication from nature, from the spirit world, a Journey of the Spirit, or a classic healing, they are all used by the shaman to better understand the worlds outside of himself. Thus he can then use this understanding to help others, to heal Earth, and enlighten us all. As a bridge, the shaman must seek spiritual help from the spirit-that-moves-in-all-things, and the worlds of spirit. He must be able to take Spiritual Journeys, to help others and also gather information for a healing. He must also use these communications to convey messages to others who cannot hear the voices beyond the flesh. All of this is part of the shaman's duty, part of the shaman's world.

The Earth Speaks

Hearing the voices of creation and of the spirit-that-moves-in-all-things, and conveying our desires to that world, is a very important aspect of the shaman's life. The shaman must be able to communicate with the world of nature to gain knowledge so that he can use that knowledge to help others or to help the various entities of nature. At first, the communication techniques will seem rather long and diffi-cult, but with continued practice the shaman will find that the communications happen very quickly and profoundly. It is like anything else that we do in life: The more we practice, the better we become at a certain skill. That is why I so often refer to these techniques as skills, for they are perfected in the same way as any other skill.

In the communications with creation we must realize one very important fact. The fact is that not all of nature has something to say to us. We may wish it to be that way, but that is just not the way it is. Nature, creation, only communicates to us when it is necessary; otherwise it remains quiet. We would soon exhaust ourselves and our patience if we tried to communicate with every entity of nature at will. We would grow very disgusted with all the failed attempts and probably abandon our spiritual path altogether. It is only when the natural world has something to say to us that we can communicate. It is important then that we remain open to all possible communication, for we never know when a voice will be sent to us. Our Inner Vision must be keenly aware of all such attempts.

When walking in the wilderness or in any natural area, the shaman should always remain open to the many voices of creation. His mind should not be cluttered with all manner of distracting outside thoughts that obscure the purity and power of nature. The shaman must be as silent and pure as possible, bringing forth the purity of the spiritual consciousness and setting aside the physical mind. It is then in the purity of this openness that we can hear the faint callings of nature through our Inner Vision. When such a voice is heard, we should then quiet ourselves even more and identify its origins. I teach my students that at this point they should clear their mind completely and pay rapt attention to the first images that appear. There can also be a deep compelling draw to some object or entity on the landscape.

Once that entity is identified and isolated, the shaman should approach it quietly and sit or recline by it if possible. It is then that the shaman should slip quietly into the Sacred Silence and end with several "breath to heart" sequences. At this point, with the eyes closed, he should bring up the image in his mind. Sometimes it is a help to physically open and close the eyes several times to help focus the image. Once the image is firmly implanted in the mind of the shaman, he asks the entity what it wants to tell him or teach him. At the point the question is asked, the shaman must let go of all thought and expectation, allowing his physical mind to go completely thoughtless. He must become pure and open to all signs, symbols, visions, and feelings conveyed to him by the entity.

Sometimes, especially when the physical mind refuses to quiet, it becomes necessary to ask the entity a series of questions that will ultimately lead to the answer. Each question is then answered by the Inner Vision, with a "no" response feeling as a tightness, and a "yes" response feeling as a release. For instance, say that you are drawn to a particular bush beside the trail. You go through all the steps of the Sacred Silence, the "breath to heart" sequence, and the point of thoughtlessness, but nothing is conveyed. You must then ask the bush if the message is for you or not. If there is no release in the Inner Vision, then you ask if the message is for someone else. You keep up this process, exhausting all of the possible questions, until there is a profound release. Once the release occurs, you have a definite starting point.

Let's say that the message was not for you but for a friend. As soon as you asked the bush if it was for a friend, you got that profound release from your Inner Vision. Now you ask the bush more questions, starting with something like if it is a medicinal message, a physical message, a need-to-know message, or some kind of other message. Now let's say that you now know that the message is on a physical level and it is something that a friend needs to know about this particular bush. With several other inquiries, paying attention to the yes and no responses, you find that this bush is very important to your friend in some way. It will ultimately help him in some way if you bring him to it. If nothing more comes, then by all means, your job is done, and you must bring your friend to the bush.

I only use the above story because it happened in exactly this way to one of my students. During an Advanced Philosophy class, Janet had just such an encounter with a bush. She also found that the bush conveyed to her exactly the fellow student that should be brought to it. She was reluctant to get the student, Frank, because the bush never told her why she must bring him to this particular location. She felt a little foolish telling him about it because she had no real definitive answer for him. He went without hesitation with Janet to the bush. They both sat for quite a while, but nothing was revealed to either of them. Janet by this time was feeling a little embarrassed and Frank a little frustrated because he felt a draw to the bush, but his Inner Vision would not reveal why.

Janet finally asked Frank if there was something he needed to know, or something he needed to do at this location. This question should have been asked in the beginning, for it would have helped them both to focus. As soon as she asked the question, the image of a watch appeared in Frank's mind, and he jumped to his feet and began searching feverishly beneath the bush. Within a few moments he uncovered the watch that he had lost several days earlier while collecting rocks for the sweatlodge. He had given it up for lost and felt so bad about losing it, for it had belonged to his grandfather. He had at one time briefly mentioned it to the class, but no one had seen it in their daily travels. It was then that Janet remembered that during the Inner Vision searching process with the bush, the roman numeral VI had appeared to her several times. She discounted it because she thought it had nothing to do with the bush. In fact, the numbers on Frank's watch were in roman numerals.

If Janet had used the symbol of the roman numeral VI when she first approached Frank, he would have probably known exactly what it was all about. The shaman must learn that all things conveyed through Inner Vision are potentially important. When the roman numeral VI came repeatedly to Janet, she should have known that it was very important in the message. After all, roman numerals are not something that people think about every day. If she still questioned its validity, then she should have gone to her Inner Vision and asked simply whether it was important or not. She would have found that her Inner Vision answered a profound "yes."

Certainly, the communication technique described above seems very long and involved, but that will quickly change with practice. By the time a student completes the third level of my philosophy workshops, the same above scenario would go something like this. Janet would have been walking by the bush when she felt spiritually drawn to its side. She would clear her mind, and the image of Frank would appear to her. The image of Frank would fade away, only to be replaced by the image of a watch lying at the base of the bush. Janet would then pick up the watch, find Frank, and give it to him. No questions asked. No surprise for either of them, for that is the way of the shaman. Surprisingly this more profound technique comes within a very short period of time and with just average practice.

Communications with the Spiritual Worlds

Communications with the world of spirit are of even more importance to the shaman than with the world of nature. The world of spirit is a vast domain of spiritual entities. Some of this world is made up of all the spiritual counterparts of our world of flesh. In other words, every entity found in our physical world can be found in the world of spirit. However, the vast majority of the spirits there are of long-departed people and entities of nature that no longer exist in our world. So, too, are there many spirits that have never been to our physical world at all. Not only does this world have all of these spiritual entities, but because it knows no time or place, it contains all history, all spiritual memory, every word ever spoken and song ever sung. It is also a place where we can view the possible and probable futures.

The shaman will use the communications with the world of spirit for many things. It can be used as a place of learning and understanding, where the shaman can go to get advice, direction, and a deeper understanding of his path. It is a place where he can receive messages to be delivered to others. It is also a place where the shaman can look back into the past or ahead into the possible and probable futures. The spirit world will also guide the shaman in a healing or direct him to do something in the physical world. Most of all it is a place where the shaman can receive guidance and direction from long-deceased realities or other powerful spirit entities. So, too, if a shaman is not careful and lacks true purpose, it can become a place of spiritual attack, where the demons from the Dark Side can get in and create havoc.

To illustrate how the communications with the spiritual world works, I want to tell you the story of Anna and her encounter with her grandfather's spirit. Anna is a middle-aged woman who lives with her two children in an old farmhouse that had been in her family for five generations. Anna lost her husband of sixteen years to cancer and now was barely able to scrape by on what she made as a secretary at a local law firm. When she came to my school, she told me that she was in danger of losing her family farm. Her small income could barely take care of her and the children, far less meet the mortgage and pay the taxes. The bank was threatening to foreclose on the land, and the government was not far behind. She could not bear the thought of losing the property that had been in her family for so many years.

During one of the first meditation exercises dealing with the journey to the Medicine Place, Anna's grandfather came to her in an image. Several times during the week, when she least expected it, her grandfather would come to her. Twice he even came in her dreams. She began to wonder if indeed she were imagining his spirit being there, as she had been very close to her grandfather, and her mind might have created his image to bring her peace. She finally asked me about it, and I told her to ask her grandfather for some kind of message. I explained to her that if her grandfather had indeed come to her so many times, unasked, then he probably had a message for her. She looked at me in a state of shock and confusion. She was surprised that I believed that the image of her grandfather was real and, more so, commonplace.

The next day Anna again saw the image of her grandfather standing before her in her Sacred Area. In her Envisioning she asked her grandfather if he had any message for her. He did not speak but grabbed a framed picture that lay beside him and showed it to her. It was a picture that she knew very well. It was an old photo of him and her grandmother sitting on the front steps of the farmhouse. The picture now lay in the back of a hall closet at the farmhouse. The image of her grandfather then pointed to the top corner of the picture as if trying to draw her attention to something. She could not exactly see what he was pointing to, and he still would not speak no matter how much she questioned him. Eventually the image of her grandfather disappeared and did not return through the remainder of the class.

Anna talked to me about her grandfather and the picture several times through the rest of the week, but she could not understand the significance of the picture. She knew the picture well and exactly where it was in the farmhouse, but she had no idea as to its importance. I told her that she would have to wait until she got home and took a good look at the picture. One thing was certain, I told her, the picture had to be important, and possibly it held a clue to something. I told her that when a spirit comes without being expected and it does something as her grandfather's spirit had done, then it is not the result of an overactive imagination but true spiritual reality. Anna seemed excited at the prospect of this possibility, yet she still held her doubts.

Less than a week after the class was over, Anna gave me a call. Her voice was both excited and shocked at what she had found. She had gone home and taken out the picture but saw nothing unusual about it. She scrutinized that area her grandfather had pointed to very carefully but still there was no clue. She resolved herself to the fact that her grandfather might just want her to hang the picture up, rather than keep it in the back of the closet. She decided then that this must be what her grandfather wanted in the first place. At this point she was disappointed, for she had hoped for more of a communication. However, in a strange way, the picture made her feel better, as if her grandfather were there with her.

Before she hung up the picture, she decided to clean up the frame and the old yellowed glass. At the kitchen table she began to remove the backing of the frame, and to her amazement she found that a corner of the frame backing was slightly bent. It was exactly the place that her grandfather had pointed to in the vision. She then carefully removed the backing. She told me that she at this point felt very spiritually excited, though she did not know why. When the back was fully removed, to her amazement she found an old envelope. Her hands shook as she opened it up. There in the envelope she found several very old IBM certificates, later to be valued at over one hundred thousand dollars. She cried as she told me this, for all of her financial problems were over, and most of all, her grandfather had helped her.

Anna's story is not unique but commonplace. The messages that come to us from the spirit world are very profound and can change our lives in a powerful way. As I stated earlier, the messages can be for us, or be delivered to someone else—it makes no difference. You will also find that the same spirits will come to you time and again with their advice and help. These spirits become as intimate as old friends and will protect and guide us through all manner of hardship, especially hardships on a spiritual level. These spirit guides are there for everyone, and it is rare for a shaman to have only one. Some guides stay with us for only a short period of time; others are there for a lifetime. It is not uncommon for a powerful spirit guide to appear to us in flesh reality, especially in times of extreme need.

Spiritual Journeys

As was told in the story of Misha's Spiritual Journey in the last chapter, the Journeys of the Spirit enable us to go to places that we cannot physically go at the time whether because of time or distance. The journeys can take us to a sick friend, to comfort a family member, or to show us something that we may need to know. At no time should a spiritual journey be taken without a very well-defined purpose, a purpose directed by Inner Vision. It is in these Spirit Journeys that we can become very vulnerable to the demons of the Dark Side. I strongly advise against taking any such journey for curiosity or practice. Nothing should be done for just the sake of practice. Instead, give the practice a more defined purpose, such as "learning to be shared with others." Remember that all Spirit Journeys must be cyclic, as stated in the previous chapter.

The Healing

Now let's look at the way that a classic "hands on" healing is accomplished, using the way Grandfather had healed the old woman as an example. It should be noted here that a shaman does not necessarily have to lay his hands on someone he is healing. The world of spirit knows no time or distance. All the shaman must do is to bring the patient to him in his or her Sacred Area and do the healing there. I find that this is the best possible way, for the patient does not realize that the shaman is healing them, and thus the spiritual identity remains a secret. As I said before, a shaman must hide the fact that he is a shaman. Grandfather was very adamant about this fact. So, too, does this keep the ego from getting involved and prevents any self-glorification.

It is only supposition as to what Grandfather really did when he helped heal the old woman, for he was well beyond my understanding. All I know is what he had taught me in the beginning. It is not what occurred on a physical level that really mattered in this healing, but what took place on the spiritual level. Probably what Grandfather did was to put the old woman on the boulder table in his Sacred Area and then place his hands on her as he did in the physical. He then prayed to the Creator to guide him and use him to facilitate this healing, stating that it was the power of the Creator and not his own that did the healing. He then imagined a tremendous source of pure white healing light lying just beneath him. This is the light and energy that would be guided through him and into the old woman.

He then must have envisioned the power of this light surging up from the envisioned Earth and into him, filling his entire body. Then he envisioned the light flowing into the old woman through his hands, filling her and driving away the blackness of the disease. He kept this circuit of light flowing for a few moments until all of the envisioned disease was washed from the old woman. So, too, was that unwavering belief that it was done. He then cut off the flow from his hands, envisioning the old woman as being still wholly filled with the light. The flow of energy was then cut from the Earth, and it left his body. This healing energy cannot be used for a shaman's personal needs. Simply, Grandfather said that a shaman must not try to heal himself, for that would be far too self-serving. The woman, as you know, was healed.

But what if Grandfather could not go to the woman on a physical level? That oftentimes is the case. The process then is the same, though there is no physical contact, only the contact with the spirit. After all, it is on the spiritual level that the healing takes place. All we need to do is to bring the person's spirit to us. I find that this is as good if not better than actual physical contact. You must understand that two people can easily get in contact with each other in the spirit world. Many of my students keep in touch with each other this way. A good example of this is with Ben and Mike.

Ben and Mike were students and partners in one of my first philosophy workshops. Ben lives in California and Mike lives in Ohio. Every week without fail they both go into the Sacred Silence on a Wednesday night at eight P.M. Pacific time and envision each other sitting and talking. On Friday nights they physically call each other to discuss what they had spiritually talked about on the Wednesday before. Without fail, year after year, they confirm exactly what they had discussed spiritually. They laugh when they tell me that this cuts down on phone bills. So you see, it is not necessary to have the patient physically in your presence, for the spiritual presence is more than enough. Remember that there is a duality of flesh and spirit. What cannot be done physically can be done spiritually, for the spirit knows no limitations.

It is important to remember here that all spiritual things must be done with an Inner Vision Direction and a purpose beyond the self. Grandfather said that we must not try to heal ourselves or our loved ones because it is too close to being self-serving. I do not try, under any circumstances, to heal myself or any of my family—I just do not take the chance.

Instead, I allow others to do it for me. So, too, any time I help heal a person, I make sure that they have exhausted all medical possibilities first, and continue with any medical procedure. We are not to be placed before modern medicine, but to help facilitate it. We are not gods, only vessels to be used by creation and the Creator.

A shaman must be able to communicate with the Earth and spirit worlds, must be able to take Spirit Journeys, and most of all, must be able to heal the Earth and its people. The communications, the journeys, and the healing must be guided by Inner Vision, have a pure purpose, a strong Sacred Silence and Envisioning process, and most of all the shaman must have a profound, unwavering belief in what he or she is doing. So, too, are we but vessels, bridges, for the life forces to flow through. It is not we who are healing, but the power of creation and the Creator. All we can ever hope to do is to be a pure and empty vessel and obey the commands given unto us.

As you know from reading this book, sharing the wilderness with Tom Brown, Jr., is a unique experience. His book and his world-famous survival school have brought a new vision to thousands. If you would like to go farther and discover more, please write for more information to:

The Tracker

Tom Brown, Tracker, Inc.
P.O. Box 927
Waretown, N.J. 08758
(609) 242-0350
www.trackerschool.com

Tracking, Nature, Wilderness Survival School